HANDGUN

HANDGUN

John Walter
Illustrated by John Batchelor

A David & Charles Military Book

British Library Cataloguing in Publication Data

Batchelor, John, *1936–*
    Handgun : from matchlock to laser-sighted
    weapon.
    1. Pistols – History
    I. Title   II. Walter, John
    683.4′32′09   TS537

    ISBN 0-7153-9172-0

© Talos Books, 1988

Printed in Portugal
for David & Charles Publishers plc
Brunel House   Newton Abbot   Devon

Distributed in the United States of America
Sterling Publishing Co., Inc.
2 Park Ave., New York, NY10016

Design by Graham Beehag
Photo research by Military Archive & Research Services

CONTENTS

Introduction

The colourful story of the handgun has its origins in the obscure history of gunpowder. Matchlocks soon led to the wheel-lock, revolutionizing cavalry tactics, and then to the perfected flinted lock early in the seventeenth century. The French Lock enjoyed unassailed popularity until, in the early nineteenth century, a clergyman in remote north-east Scotland adapted unstable fulminates to a gunlock.

Forsyth's percussion lock, capricious and delicate, inspired the percussion cap; it paved the way for Samuel Colt, gloriously decorative examples of whose guns celebrate the company's recent sesquicentennial; and it facilitated the mass slaughter of the American Civil War, where the domination of nineteenth-century weaponry over seventeenth-century tactics was punched home by battlefield photography.

By proving the worth of metallic cartridges, the Civil War also allowed Smith & Wesson a monopoly that lasted until Colt produced the classic 'Peacemaker' in 1873. The European revolver, however, was soon challenged by automatic pistols such as the Borchardt, the Mauser and the first Brownings. These appealed so greatly that virtually all of the modern operating systems had been perfected by 1914.

As the story of the pistol is not merely that of the successes, oddities such as the Elgin Pistol-Cutlass, the Cochran Monitor turret gun and the Bechtler Double-end Pistol will be found here alongside the modern magnums. Yet it is impossible to record the entire history of the pistol in any one book, and my debt must be acknowledged to the many authors whose work I consulted – particularly Howard Blackmore, Claude Blair, Edward Ezell, Frank Sellers and Anthony Taylerson, together with the late George Nonte, Lewis Winant, Samuel E. Smith and Walter H.B. Smith, all of whom are survived by a valuable legacy. I would particularly like to thank Ian Hogg, whose friendship and assistance have been invaluable, and last – but not least – John Batchelor, whose meticulous illustrations *are* this book.

John Walter   Hampden Park, Eastbourne, 1988

Displaying such patriotic motifs as George Washington and the Liberty Bell, this ornate Colt Dragoon replica was auctioned at the 1976 National Sporting Goods Association Convention. It fetched $55,000.

1. From Fire and Brimstone

It was a pity, so 'twas,
This villainous saltpetre should be digg'd
Out of the bowels of the harmless earth,
Which many a good tall fellow had destroy'd
So cowardly; and but for these vile guns,
He would himself have been a soldier.

William Shakespeare (*c*.1564-1616), *Henry IV*, Part I, Act I, iii.

There could be no modern handgun without the discovery that an explosive could be made from the constituents of the incendiary 'Greek Fire'. Precisely where, when and how this happened is still a matter for dispute, as evidence from such a far-off time – perhaps understandably – is conspicuous by its absence.

Long before the introduction of gunpowder, incendiaries compounded from pitch, charcoal, fat and sulphur sputtered and flamed for the Greeks, Romans, Arabs and Chinese. It is easy to see how the discovery of the explosive qualities of a mix of saltpetre, charcoal and sulphur could have arisen unexpectedly had an experimenter enclosed his mixture in a stout jar. This provides an insight into the legend of 'Black Berthold', supposedly based on Constantin Anglitzen, a Franciscan monk living in Freiburg im Breisgau in the mid-fourteenth century. Berthold, the story relates, was so wary of the basilisk – a mythical serpent alchemists believed to inhabit mercury – that he sought to protect himself in his desire to transmute mercury to gold. Supposing that a mixture of hot sulphur and cool saltpetre would so confuse the basilisk that it would consume itself, Berthold was nearly killed in the explosion as he mixed the ingredients in his mortar.

The story is entertaining, but has no basis in reality. No modern researcher has proved Berthold's existence outside legend, and the most reliable source dates his discoveries to 1393. As the earliest known depiction of a cannon antedates 1326, and as a powder manufactory was active in Augsburg as early as 1340, the claims of 'Black Berthold' can be dismissed.

In 1242, an English Franciscan monk named Roger Bacon (*c*.1214-94) is said to have written his now-lost tract *De Mirabili Potestate Artis et Naturae* ('On the marvellous power of art and nature'), in which he revealed the composition of gunpowder in the form of an anagram. A seventeenth century transcription of a later treatise, *De Secretis Operibus Artis et Naturae et de Nullitae Magiae*, usually dated to *c*.1248 but more probably dating from 1257-67, repeats the formula. Unfortunately, this is not included in

A fifteenth-century war chariot, in which matchlocks co-exist with the bow.

the only known thirteenth-century example of Bacon's work, and a fifteenth century version in the British Museum reads very differently. The popular transcription of the relevant passage from *Opus Tertius*, generally agreed to date in its original form from 1268, is ' . . . of saltpetre take seven parts, five of young hazel-twigs, and five of sulphur; and so shall you call up the power of thunder and destruction, if you know the art.' However, it has been questioned whether the translator, Colonel H.W.L. Hine in his book *Gunpowder and Ammunition, their Origin and Progress*, published

This three-barrel Korean hand gun is typical of the earliest hand-held firearms.

in London in 1904, merely saw in Bacon's manuscript what he wanted to find.

There is no evidence that Bacon discovered the short step from incendiary compound to true gunpowder, though he clearly understood its explosive potential. He also seems to have been aware that purer potassium nitrate (saltpetre) could be obtained by crystallisation from hot water, rather than through the traditional methods of scraping it from walls or preparing it from urine-sodden mounds of earth, animal refuse and wood-ash. The Arab scholar Ḥaṣan al-Rammāh, quoting earlier authors, was describing an efficient saltpetre purification process as early as 1280 and it is probable that the secret had been known as much as fifty years previously.

It is often suggested that the secrets of gunpowder were brought to Europe by way of China and Arabia, but neither case is proven. Champions of the Chinese claim point to the existence of the *Wu Ching Ts'ung Yao* (allegedly dating from 1044) in which, however, the identification of gunpowder has probably been confused with an incendiary mixture. Though references to bamboo-tube guns or Huo-ch'iang occur many times between 1130 and 1233, the oldest probably refers simply to 'roman candles' loaded with alternating layers of sticky incendiary mixture and proto-gunpowder. Mention of a 'bomb of pig iron' (1221) and what could be interpreted as a true bullet- or arrow-firing bamboo gun (1259) suggests that gunpowder appeared in China towards the end of the Sung dynasty (960-1279) and then travelled comparatively quickly to Europe through Arab traders.

Once the explosive properties of gunpowder had been appreciated, it was but a small step to the first gun. *De*

The surrender of a medieval city. Note the bombard in the background.

Nobilitatibus, Sapientiis et Prudentiis Regum, a Latin tutorial prepared by Walter de Milemete for Prince Edward a year prior to the latter's accession to the throne of England in 1327, illustrates the earliest datable gun. As an undated manuscript from the same hand has been tentatively identified from *c*.1322, it is probable that cannon were known in England as early as 1320; and, as two men were appointed to make lead bullets, arrows and metal cannon in Florence in 1326-27, the advent of guns may be retraceable to the end of the thirteenth century. According to the historian Thomas F. Tout, in his article 'Firearms in England in the Fourteenth Century' (*English Historical Review*, October 1911), an entry in the Privy Wardrobe accounts for 1345 mentions repairs to 'old' guns.

The curious de Milemete 'pot-de-fer' gun (i.e., shaped like an iron pot) is shown firing an arrow, a somewhat alarmed-looking knight wielding a lighted brand with which the charge has been ignited. The painted colours are unnatural, and it is unlikely that the fletching was mere feathers. Later evidence suggests that the arrows were sealed by wrapping the shafts with tallowed cloth or greased leather straps.

Pots-de-fer were made by traditional bell-founding methods, which would undoubtedly have given them considerable strength; the bore was a short, small-diameter cylinder bored from the muzzle and communicating with the narrow flash-hole channel in the breech. Neither the de Milemete tutorial (now in the Library of Christ Church, Oxford) nor the undated *De Secretis Secretorum* in the British Museum, which illustrate small and large pots-de-fer respectively, show any special mounting: guns were either laid on a table or supported on trestles. This is usually assumed to be artists' licence, but, as the concept of accuracy meant little at the time, backward movement of the cannon body on its support may simply have been accepted as normal. As the projectiles were substantially lighter than the gun, and taking into the account friction between the gun and the supports, the recoil velocity would have been relatively low and the distance of travel commensurately small.

The intention behind the earliest cannon seems to have been to terrify rather than destroy. In this they succeeded admirably. Edward III (1327-77) is said to have taken 'crakys of war' on his earliest incursions into Scotland, pots-de-fer were used at the siege of Cividale in 1331, and the English allegedly had four cannon at the battle of Crécy (1346). Here, the noise and smoke from the cannon, quite apart from the devastating rain of arrows from the English archers, panicked the mercenary Genoese crossbowmen straight back into the path of the French knights. The latter unsportingly carved their way through the luckless Italians before learning that even they had no answer to an iron-tipped clothyard shaft from the bow of an English yeoman.

By the time of Crécy, the constituents of gunpowder – seven parts saltpetre, five each of sulphur and charcoal according to Roger Bacon – had become two-thirds saltpetre, two-ninths charcoal and one-ninth of sulphur. This gave better power and less smoke, but quality was still very poor. Not only were the sulphur and saltpetre

The siege of La Roche -Île from a fifteenth-century manuscript.

impure, but the mixture had a tendency to separate during transport and required re-mixing by the gunner. As gunpowder is notoriously sensitive to friction, many a man lost a hand, an arm or even his life in the service of his art.

Though continual improvements were made in the composition of the explosive, which had all but reached the accepted modern proportions by the end of the seventeenth century, the earlier discovery of 'corned' gunpowder represented the greatest single technological advance. The basic constituents were mixed with a little water and the resulting paste was sieved, allowed to dry naturally and then packed; provided the concoction remained moist during the sieving, premature explosions were greatly reduced. Corned powder gave much less smoke and burned more evenly than its predecessor, permitting greater power for a given charge weight.

Compared with bore size, the pot-de-fer was unnecessarily wasteful of valuable metal. Its successor was the cannon, the term apparently deriving from the medieval Italian word 'canna' ('reed'). The earliest cannon were constructed by beating strips of wrought iron around a wooden mandrel until the seams between the strips were strong enough to withstand the force of explosion. Once the forging had been completed, wrought iron reinforcing hoops were shrunk onto the barrel and the mandrel was drilled out to form the bore.

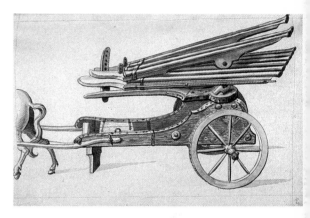

A large ribauld or 'Death's Organ', from a sixteenth-century manuscript.

Unfortunately, manufacturing standards were very erratic and, though the best guns were capable of withstanding years of use, many were capricious. For example, 'Mons Meg', the large bombard now displayed in Edinburgh Castle, was forged c.1450 either in Ghent, Edinburgh Castle or the Stewartry of Kirkcudbright, and survived periodic use until the barrel split while firing a salute on the birthday of the Duke of York in 1680; it was ironic that James II of Scotland, who may have used Mons Meg to help smash the rebellious Douglasses of Threave Castle, met his death in August 1460 when 'The Lion' exploded at the siege of Roxburgh Castle.

Though most early cannon were large – often gargantuan – even their most enthusiastic champions appreciated that they were restricted to siege and static warfare. Consequently, smaller guns were useful for local defence or to repel mass attacks; among the earliest of these was the multi-barrelled Orgue, Orgelgeschütz, Ribauld or Ribaldequin. Most barrel-sets were parallel, mounted either on a static wooden bed or a stout-wheeled carriage, though a few examples were slightly splayed to increase the arc of fire. Apart from an occasional excessively large and clumsy example (one was more than twenty feet high and had three superimposed ranks of barrels), the ribauld soon proved the merits of mobility.

Soon, each of the barrels was taken from the wooden bed, stocked or hafted individually, and issued to one man – who could then select targets with much greater freedom than the crew of the ribauld, which was easily outflanked. Thus appeared the earliest handgun, a phrase which initially referred to a shoulder arm. The oldest known example dates from the middle of the fourteenth century. It is safe to assume that the first such weapons date earlier than 1350 as, according to Tout, 'guns with tillers' – 'tiller' then being synonymous with a crossbow stock – were inventoried in England as early as 1345.

Though their construction varies, most surviving pre-1450 handguns were affixed to an elongated wood bed by rope or iron bands, had a socket into which a pole could be inserted, or a spike that could be driven into a haft. Others had twisted wrought-iron barrel extensions, generally ending in a ring or knob. Most are quite small – the .65 calibre Swedish Mörkö Gun has a barrel measuring 7.6in, while that of the .70 calibre Tannenberg Gun is nearer twelve – and the bores are rarely greater than an inch. Excavated from the ruins of a German castle destroyed in 1399, the Tannenberg Gun weighs a little less than three pounds without its stock (cf., early wheel-lock pistols at 5lb or more).

Hot coal, a tinder-stick or a smouldering brand were applied to the flash-hole to fire the gun, but accuracy would have been very bad. The poor quality of contemporary gunpowder necessitated filling more than half the barrel; and this, with the interposition of a wooden sabot ahead of the charge, allowed the ball very little movement before emerging from the muzzle. The earliest handguns, therefore, were ultra-short range weapons fired either by placing the stock on the shoulder – like the modern bazooka grip – or by clamping it beneath in the armpit and, when possible, bracing the stock-tip against the ground. At this stage in firearms history, effect still counted for more than efficiency.

Gunfounding techniques gradually improved, reducing accidental barrel-bursts; hooks were added beneath the barrel to minimise recoil by bracing the hook against a castle wall, a tree-bough or even an earthen bank; rudimentary sights were added; and the shapes of the stock were refined. The first major advance, however, was the appearance of the matchlock.

Below: **A typically ornate Japanese matchlock, examples of which were still being made in the 1850s.**

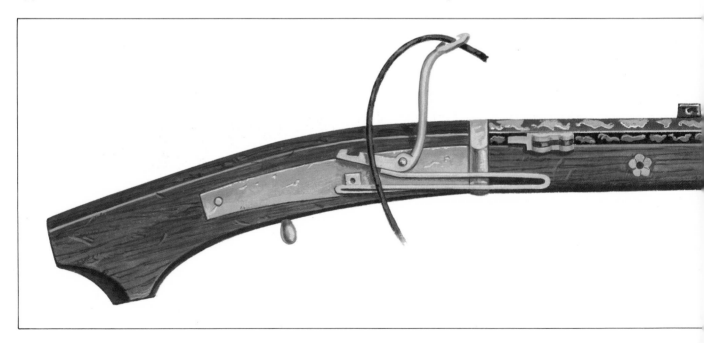

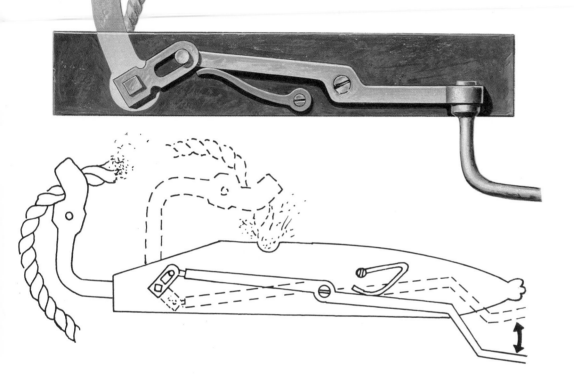

Below: When the trigger bar of a 'primitive matchlock' is pressed, the link drops the cock against the pressure of its spring.

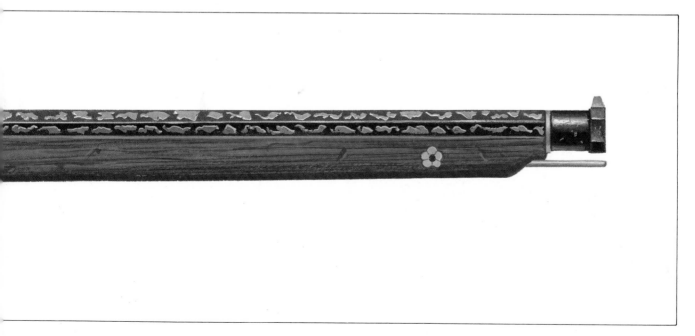

All that can be said with certainty is that the matchlock had appeared by the time of the Hussite Wars (1420-34), the earliest known illustration being dated 1411. The first handguns had been ignited simply by sprinkling powder into a small central depression above the flash-hole, but this prevented the gunner viewing the target and the touch-hole soon moved to the right side of the barrel. A ledge was added to retain the powder, and then a slow-burning match was developed to aid the gunner's work. However, as he still had to concentrate on his gun rather than his target, a more appropriate means of applying match to powder was badly needed.

By the end of the fifteenth century, the lock had been modified so that the match was clamped in the jaws of an arm designed to lower the match unerringly into the pan. The mechanism initially used an extension bar or 'tricker' protruding below the stock, where it could be grasped with a stock-supporting hand; this connected directly to the match-cock, which was simply lowered as the tricker-bar was pressed. Later examples – known as 'snapping matchlocks' – incorporated a spring and an intermediate sear. The match sprang into the pan once the tricker-bar was pressed beyond a certain point; however, as the tricker-bar was still directly connected to the match-holder, these guns could fire prematurely if the bar was struck accidentally. Within eighty years, they had been supplemented by the 'trigger matchlock', in which a conventional trigger, complete with guard, released the spring-loaded match-lever only after the latter had been cocked.

Though not without their own peculiar problems – for example, the match could be extinguished by the force of impact in the pan – guns of this type remained popular throughout most of the sixteenth century and, being cheap and easily repaired, were still to be found in standing armies as late as the English Civil War (1642-8). Their influence had been world-wide. A hundred years previously, in 1543, the first matchlock-carrying Portuguese traders had landed on the Japanese island of Tanegashima and so impressed Lord Takitaka that an onlooker left a memorable description of the incredulity of someone who had never previously seen a gun: 'In their hands they carried something two or three feet long . . . with a passage inside. Its shape defies comparison with anything I know. To use it, fill it with powder and small lead pellets. Set up a small white target on a bank. Grip the object in your hand, compose your spirit and, closing one eye, apply fire to the fire-hole. Thus the pellet hits the target squarely. The explosion is like lightning and the report like thunder . . .'

By a heady mix of purchase and seduction, the Japanese mastered the art of gunfounding so quickly that snapping matchlocks were being mass-produced by 1550. Rather perversely, such guns remained the principal firearm found in that isolated oriental land until the re-opening of Japan by the American Matthew Perry (1853) and the eventual supersession of the Tokugawa shogunate by an imperial restoration in 1868. Like the samurai sword, the matchlocks had been held in such a strange veneration that practically no mechanical development had occurred. For many

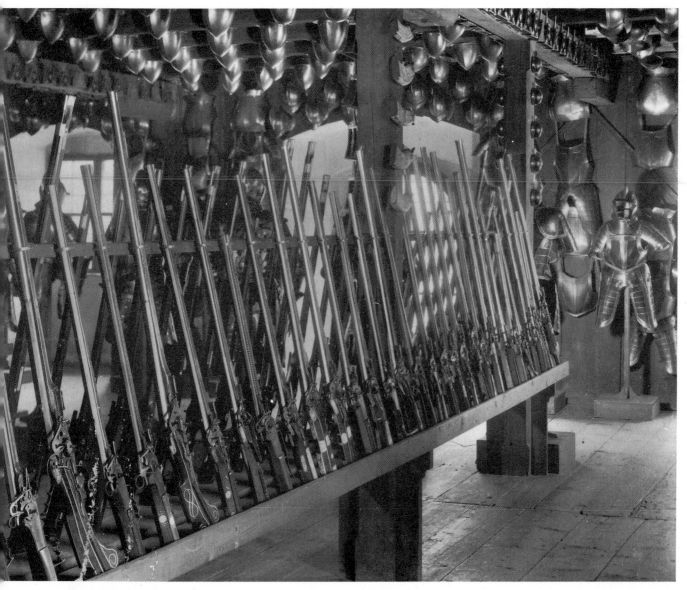

This view of the Steiermärkisches
Landeszeughaus, Graz, gives a good
impression of a medieval armoury.

years they had even been christened 'Tanegashima' after the island
on which they were first seen, though now more commonly labelled
'fire-rope guns' (hinawa-jū).

The development of an effectual matchlock broadened the
handgun's appeal; the stock was greatly refined, taking a form that
is instantaneously recognisable as a gun even today, trigger-guards
and tube-sights were added, and the matchlock arquebus became
acceptable for military service. Though performance depended on
keeping the slow-match alight through wind and rain, and though its
range, accuracy and fire-rate were all vastly inferior to the longbow,
the gun was much more easily mastered. Training an archer took
years, whereas the rudiments of gunnery came easily to even the
most obtuse medieval peasantry. And enough peasants, provided
they had powder and ammunition, could defeat even the lordliest
knight. At a stroke, war had become democratic; rank and class no
longer guaranteed chivalrous treatment, and a king could indeed be
killed by a commoner.

2. Seeking Perfection

And since an especially dangerous kind of firearm has come to be used . . . , His Excellency, knowing that these are devilish arms, prohibits their being carried . . . under penalty of having a hand publicly cut off.

Ducal decree, Ferrara, Italy, 1523

Being simple and robust, the matchlock was admirably suited to military use, but inefficient enough to inspire further experimentation. The first tangible result was the wheel-lock, in which a wedge of iron pyrites was held against a serrated wheel rotated by a spring connected to the wheel-spindle by a short chain. Each time the gun was to be fired, a special key was placed over a spindle protruding through the centre of the wheel and the mechanism was 'spanned'. The wheel-spindle was turned until the trigger engaged the sear and the gun was ready for action. It still required a panful of fine-grain priming powder, but ignition was immeasurably better than the uncertain glowing match of its predecessors. Owing to the closed pan and the provision of sparks from mineral rubbing on metal, the wheel-lock could fire in wind or even light rain; for the first time, a gun could be carried loaded at all times. Neither did it give away the firer's position – before the shot, at least – as a lighted match had done.

The wheel-lock could be loaded and primed, and then readied for action merely by spanning the wheel, opening the pan and setting the cock; if the opportunity passed, the pan could be closed, the cock withdrawn and the trigger pressed to release the wheel. On the debit side, pyrites were soft, had a short life and often disintegrated in the cock-jaws.

The wheel-lock is traditionally credited to Johann Kiefuss, a Nuremburg clockmaker, and there is little doubt that the wheel-lock owes much to contemporary clock escapements; as clockmaking and gunsmithing were often closely related in these early days, the wheel-lock probably did originate in southern Germany. However, Leonardo da Vinci, in *Codex Atlanticus*, illustrates a tinder lighter and a gun-lock of rudimentary wheel type. In recent years, both have been successfully reconstructed from da Vinci's drawings. Unfortunately, *Codex Atlanticus* was prepared over many years, has been rearranged at some time past, and is difficult to date. Leonardo's wheel-lock system has been assessed as 'not later than ten years' prior to his death in 1519; 1505-10 seems reasonable, but

Right: A special spanner was needed to turn the wheel of the wheel-lock until it engaged the sear.

Below: A typical Italian wheel-lock pistol, *c.*1640.

claims as early as 1482-99 have also been made. The significance of the *Codex Atlanticus* drawings hinges on a similar illustration by Martin Löffelholz of Nuremburg, which is dated 1505; who copied whom . . . ? By 1507, a wheel-lock had been ordered for the bishop of Zagreb and references thereafter multiply rapidly. The oldest known survivor – by Bartholomäus Marquardt of Nuremburg – is dated 1530. Surviving examples are invariably well made, though not always well designed, and often show decoration of the highest quality.

The wheel-lock had such obvious advantages that it was soon being made in large numbers. Most of the earliest guns were made in southern Germany and Bohemia, though Italian examples were being made by 1522. Gradually, the principles spread throughout Europe in the middle of the sixteenth century; however, only one English gun has yet been identified. As the mechanism was complicated compared with the primitive matchlock, manufacture – even of the plainest military grades – was confined to skilled gunsmith-clockmakers. In addition, the expense of the wheel-lock confined it largely to noblemen or specialist military units. The Reiter (light cavalry) galloped up to the enemy, fired their saddle pistols at close range, and then retired to reload. This tactic proved effectual time and time again, until the intended victims realised that Reiter were vulnerable to counter-attack while reloading.

Minor changes were made to the wheel-lock throughout the sixteenth century. Few of these affected the basic function, but attempts were made to provide two cocks in case one broke; double barrels or superimposed loads; enclosed locks; and refinements to accelerate ignition. One enterprising French gunsmith, Pierre

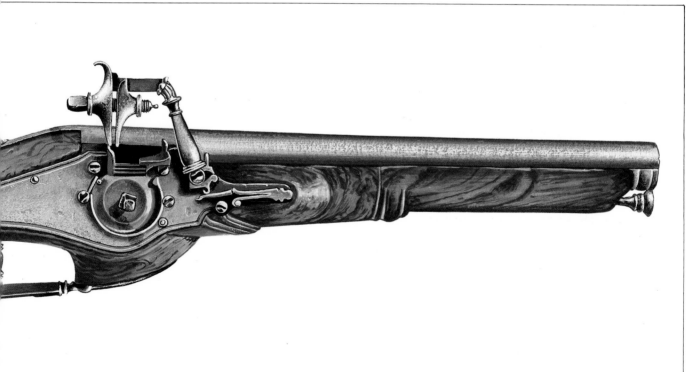

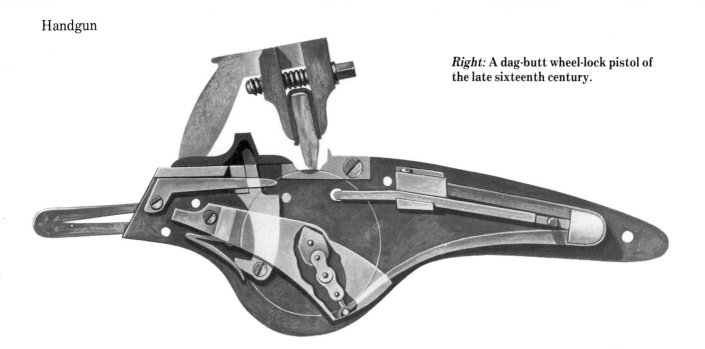

Right: **A dag-butt wheel-lock pistol of the late sixteenth century.**

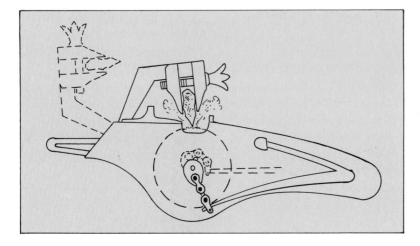

Above and left: **The interior of a wheel-lock, showing the short chain that rotated the wheel.**

Bergier of Grenoble, even constructed a genuinely waterproof wheel-lock for presentation to Louis XIII of France in about 1631. This *tour de force* he subsequently topped with a four-shot superimposed-load wheel-lock arquebus, and a brace of two-shot pistols followed in 1634. By this time, however, the importance of the wheel-lock was declining in the face of increasing competition from the flintlock, though the last wheel-lock pistols – a fine-quality brace made by Le Page of Paris, 'Armurier du Roi' (armourer to the king) – were not made until 1829.

Arquebus or musket-length wheel-locks are comparatively rare, apart from Tschinke. These northern European sporting guns show an extraordinary lightness of construction, externally borne lockwork and uncomfortable-looking stocks adapted to the bizarre habit of firing with the butts above the shoulder. Most surviving wheel-lock 'shoulder' arms are petronels (from the French *poitrine*, 'chest'), so called because their distinctive sharply-curved butts rested against the chest-piece of the firer's armour. Others are dags, massive carbines intended to be fired with one hand; and the many

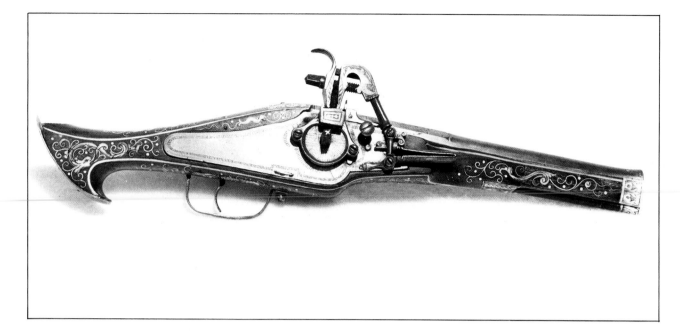

true pistols vary from hefty military weapons, carried in saddle holsters, to jewels of the miniaturists' art.

Wheel-lock pistols are the first true handguns, few previous guns being capable of one-hand operation. The word 'pistol' is believed to have come not from the Italian town-name Pistoia, but from the Bohemian noun 'pištal' – a [smoker's] pipe, the shape of which, when inverted, greatly resembled the early military wheel-locks. The word 'pistol' is first recorded in English in 1570, but had achieved currency early in the succeeding century.

By the last quarter of the sixteenth century, the wheel-lock was well tried and tested. It was efficient but expensive, and cheaper solutions were already being sought. The first was the snaphance, the term deriving from the Dutch 'Snaphaan' ('pecking chicken'). It described the action concisely. The designers had recognised in the softness of iron pyrites a considerable risk to ignition and had substituted hard flint, the sparking qualities of which had been known for millenia. The snaphance or Dutch lock was set by retracting the cock, the spindle of which ran through a tumbler on the inside of the lock-plate. The tumbler bore on the mainspring and a laterally-moving sear intercepted the tail of the hammer through an aperture in the lock-plate. The cock held a flint wedge in its jaws. The steel was then pulled down to its rearmost position. When the trigger was pulled, the cock flew forwards – opening the pan cover – and struck the steel; the latter, pivoted by the impact, then rose forward under spring pressure and showered sparks into the pan from the serrated steel-face.

The method was more effectual than the wheel-lock and appreciably cheaper to make; consequently, it soon attained popularity in north-western Europe, especially in Holland, parts of Italy, England and Scotland. The laterally-moving sear presented something of a problem, however, as a satisfactory half-cock position was difficult to achieve. Once the sear-hole in the cock or the nose of

Below: **A sixteenth-century antler-body powder flask.**

the sear began to wear, the cock displayed a distressing tendency to slip. Even if the steel was properly emplaced, however, the gun could only fire from full-cock. Slipping from intermediate positions was insufficient to rotate the steel and nothing of note happened: the gun had, in fact, 'gone off at half-cock'.

Dutch Lock guns made in England in the period immediately preceding the Civil War (1642-8) often have the pan cover and the steel combined into a 'frizzen'. This reduced the safety factor and manufacturing complexity equally; consequently, the English gunmakers added a catch (or 'dog') on the lock-plate to hold the cock at full-cock. The earlier English snaphance is usually known as an 'English Lock'; the later variant, not surprisingly, as a Dog Lock.

The Scots accepted the true snaphance almost without modification, the regional distinction being evident in typically Celtic scrollwork rather than construction. Inexplicably, the Scots had an aversion to woodwork and trigger guards; though some of the earliest guns display both these features, the classically Scottish pistol features all-steel (more rarely, all-brass) construction, a ball-type trigger and a small pricker in the butt. Butts are now generally classed by shape – as scroll or ram's horn, lemon or ovate, heart or kidney – and the unmistakable style lasted well into the flintlock era. Most of the best Scottish pistols emanated from Doune in Perthshire, where, according to the *Statistical Account of Scotland . . .* (1798), the art of making Highland pistols 'was introduced . . . about the year 1646, by Thomas Caddell, who, having been instructed in his craft at Muthill, a village in Strathearn in Perthshire, came and settled . . .'

Dutch Lock guns made in Scandinavia are also most distinctive, with long slender cocks not unlike those of the snapping matchlocks they replaced. The pan cover is often combined with the steel, as in the English Lock, and, inspired by the Tschinke, the mainspring is generally fitted externally.

While the Dutch Lock reigned supreme in most of Europe, with the occasional excursion into northern Italy, an alternative flinted lock was developed in the south. The evidence, which includes a Florentine reference to 'flint guns' datable to 1547, suggests that the pattern originated in Italy and then migrated to Spain. The principal recognition features of this Mediterranean or Spanish Lock are the combined pan and steel, a distinctively shaped cock (known as a 'dog' in southern Europe), a laterally acting sear without a tumbler, and a sturdy external mainspring.

The spring usually presses downward on the toe of the dog in Italian-made locks, but upward on the dog-heel on Spanish examples. The perfection of the latter is generally credited to Simon Marquarte the Younger, who worked between 1585 and 1640, lending credence to the claim that the Spanish Lock came to the Iberian Peninsula from Italy. The popular name for these locks, Miquelet, was fancifully derived in the nineteenth century from the Pyrenean bandits called Los Miqueletos; the original Spanish term 'Llave patilla', or 'foot-lock', derived from the distinctive shape of the base of the cock.

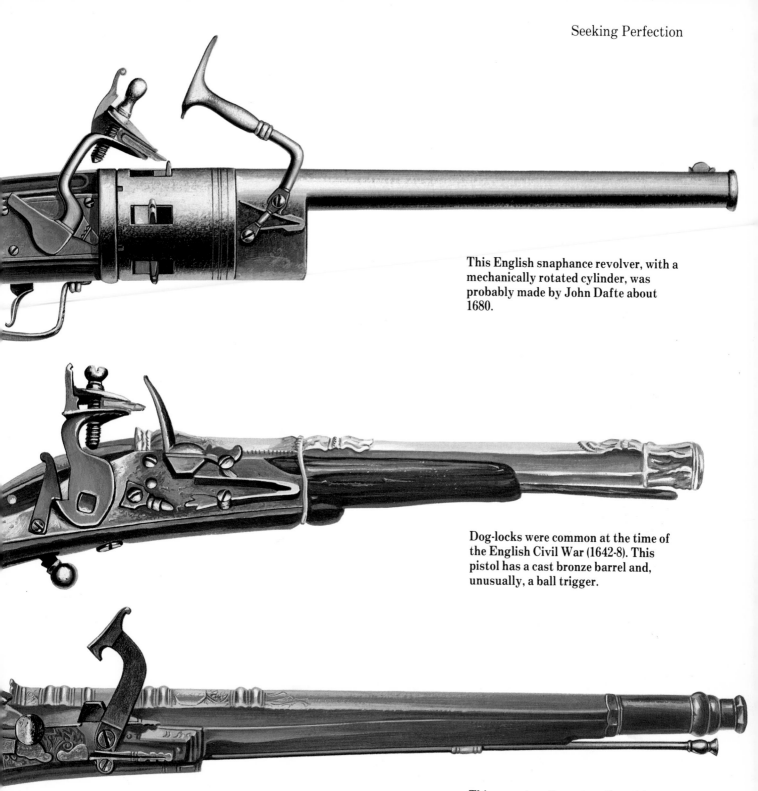

This English snaphance revolver, with a mechanically rotated cylinder, was probably made by John Dafte about 1680.

Dog-locks were common at the time of the English Civil War (1642-8). This pistol has a cast bronze barrel and, unusually, a ball trigger.

This seventeenth-century Scottish snaphance pistol displays a fishtail butt and typical scrollwork decoration.

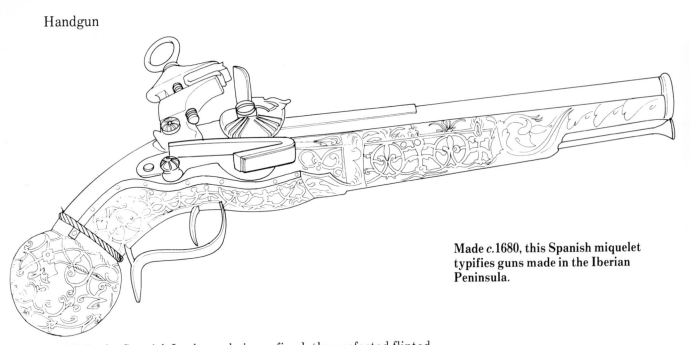

Made *c*.1680, this Spanish miquelet typifies guns made in the Iberian Peninsula.

While the Spanish Lock was being refined, the perfected flinted lock appeared in France. Its 'inventor' is universally agreed to be Marin le Bourgeoys (*c*.1550-1638), painter and Valet de Chambre to Henri IV and Louis XIII. Nothing is particularly innovative about the first French Lock, which appeared about 1612-15, as it merely combined the one-piece frizzen of the Spanish Lock and the general construction of the Dutch Lock (snaphance) with one major contribution of its own – the vertically moving sear. In purely mechanical terms, this is appreciably less important than the progression from the matchlock to the wheel-lock. Neither is it as important as the advance from the flintlock to the percussion lock, which resulted from major advances in chemistry. However, the vertically moving sear in the French Lock provided a reliable cocking action and, for the first time, an effectual half-cock feature; in addition, wear in the sear or tumbler was much less worrying than in preceding lock designs.

Once the French Lock had been established, by the 1630s, most subsequent improvements concerned construction rather than basic principles. Though virtually all longarms had massive sidelocks,

A Spanish Lock or 'Miquelet'. Note the laterally-moving sear.

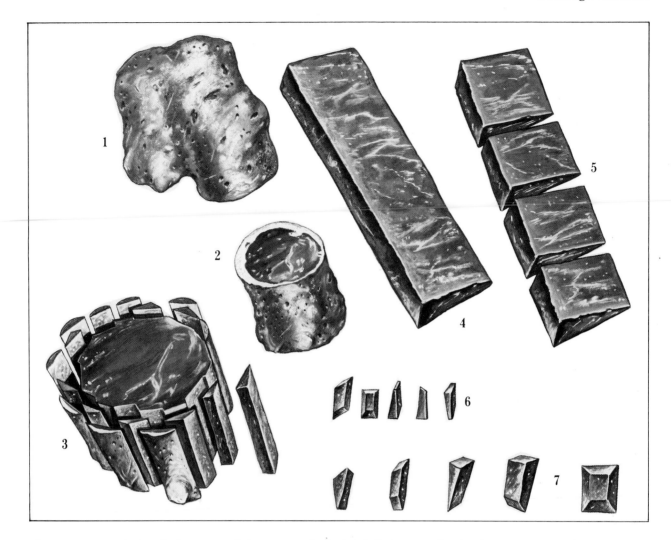

these were so obviously inappropriate on a pocket pistol that an efficient box-lock – with the hammer carried centrally – was subsequently perfected in England. Thereafter, an infinite number of variations was produced on the flintlock pistol theme: large-bore military holster pistols, generally plain and sturdy; carriage and coach pistols, cased in pairs to protect a traveller from the ravages of highwaymen; small pistols to be concealed in a gentleman's pocket or lady's muffler; multi-barrel or multi-shot pistols to increase fire-rate; pistols fitted with folding bayonets, such as that patented by John Waters of Birmingham in 1781; breechloading pistols designed in pursuit of accuracy – the list is practically endless. The most effectual were the elegant duelling pistols, the apogee of flintlock development.

The English duelling pistol presents a fascinating story in itself, from the first refined holster pistols of 1770 – with its cannon barrel and brass mounts – to the saw-handled iron-mounted guns of the first quarter of the nineteenth century, whose browned non-reflecting finish, micro-groove rifling (rifled barrels were theoretically frowned on by English duellists) and swamped octagonal barrels were all designed for efficiency at the expense of show. Though a breach of King's Regulations, to refuse a challenge

Production of a gunflint. 1, the flint; 2, the trimmed or 'knapped' original; 3, separating the blades; 4, an individual blade; 5, separating the gunflints; 6, the rough gunflints; and 7, the finished article.

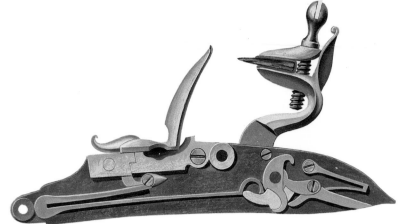

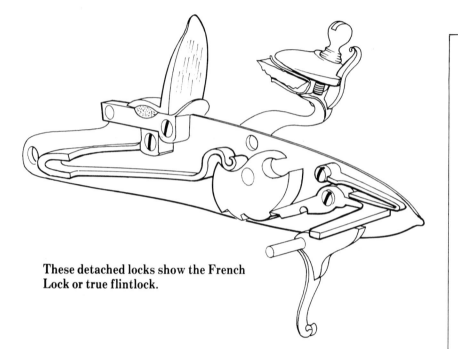

These detached locks show the French Lock or true flintlock.

A pair of good-quality English holster pistols by Griffin, London, 1765.

was often regarded as cowardice in the British Army; countless deaths, flights from justice and needless persecution resulted until the practice was finally stamped out in 1844. But there had been some famous encounters: in May 1789, a ball fired from a Wogdon flintlock dueller by Lieutenant-Colonel Charles Lennox of the Coldstream Guards narrowly missed the head of the Duke of York, undoubtedly the closest any member of the British Royal Family brushed with death in a duel. Even as late as 1829, the Duke of Wellington met the Earl of Winchilsea at Battersea Fields to settle a quarrel.

Regional variations are as evident among French Locks as in the earlier Dutch patterns, though the changes usually concern the stock arrangements rather than the lock itself. Excluding the military pistols, which generally follow a single recognisable pattern, the most distinctive flintlocks are the all-metal Scottish guns. French guns of the post-Revolutionary period may be characterised by their butts, which are generally more angular than contemporary round-butt English patterns and often end in a short

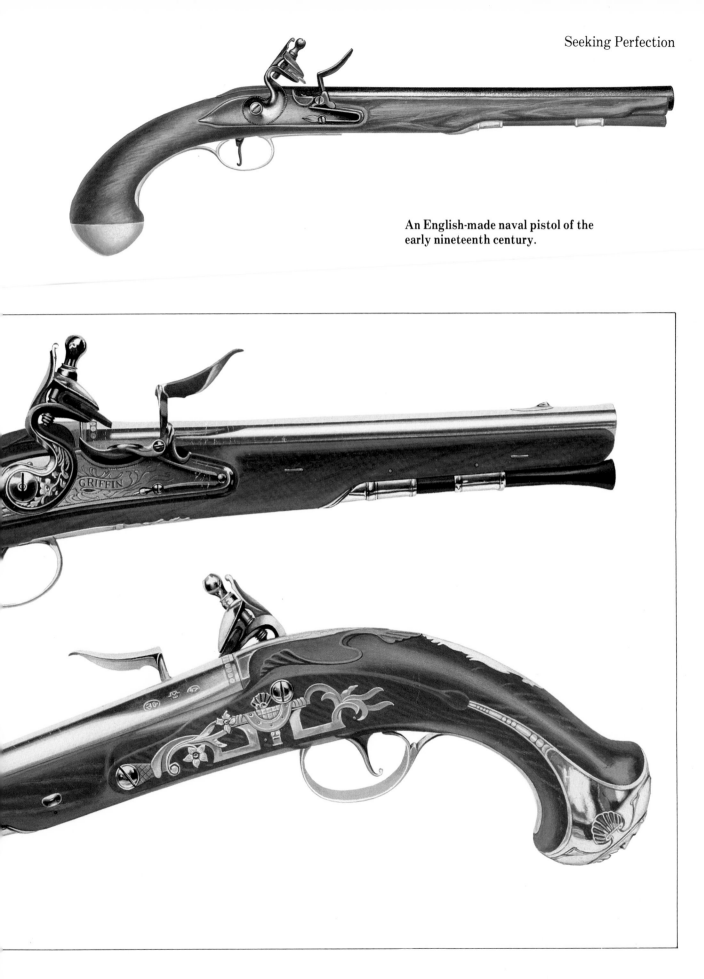

An English-made naval pistol of the early nineteenth century.

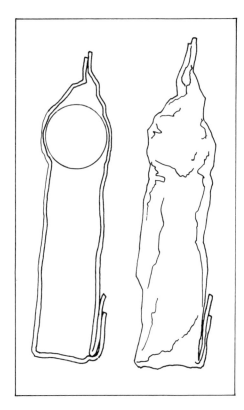

Normally associated with military muskets, paper cartridges could also be supplied with pistols and, particularly, percussion revolvers.

flat pommel. The finest examples made during Napoleon's First Empire and the early years of the Bourbon Restoration, particularly by Nicolas-Noël Boutet and Le Page, are often decorated in an excessively grandiose style and are cased in French manner – with each part set in a contoured recess rather than the English style of partitioning.

French pistols, excepting those produced during the immediately post-Revolutionary period, reflect a rich taste fuelled by such fashionable designs as the pattern books of Etienne Delaune (c.1519-88), who influenced the German master Sädeler; *Livre de diverses Ordonnances, du Feuillages, Moresques* by Thomas Picquot (published in 1638); and *Plusieurs Pièces et autres Ornements pour les Arquebusiers* by Claude and Jacques Simonin, published c.1693 and based on 'the best Parisian work'. Later works included de la Collombe's (c.1704); and *Nouveaux Desseins d'Arquebuserie* by Claude Gillot, who died in 1722.

Italian flintlocks are often most distinctive, reflecting a tradition that found its best expression in the work of the Brescian smith Lazarino Cominazzo (d.1696) and his pupils. The guns are generally lighter and more elegant than northern European products, and, particularly when of good quality, display rich decoration in the form of precisely pierced and chiselled tracery.

This trooper of the King's Dragoon Guards, painted c.1751, brandishes a holster pistol typical of the period.

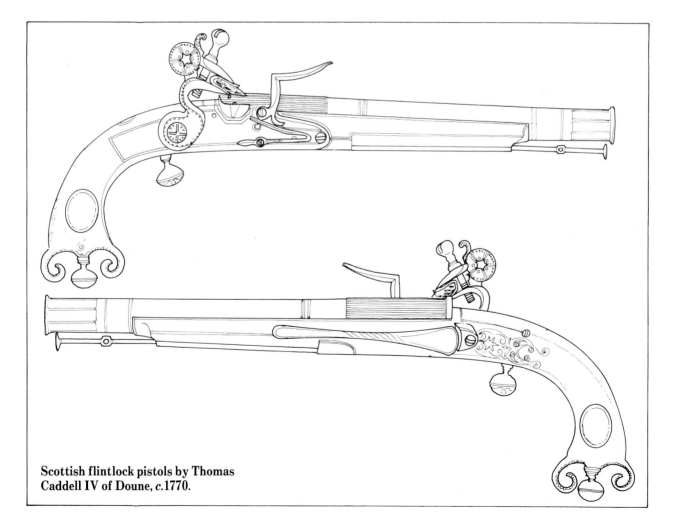

One of a pair of duelling pistols by McDermott of Dublin about 1812, owned by the famous Irish politician Daniel O'Connell. The French-style recurved cock and waterproof pans are notable.

Scottish flintlock pistols by Thomas Caddell IV of Doune, *c.*1770.

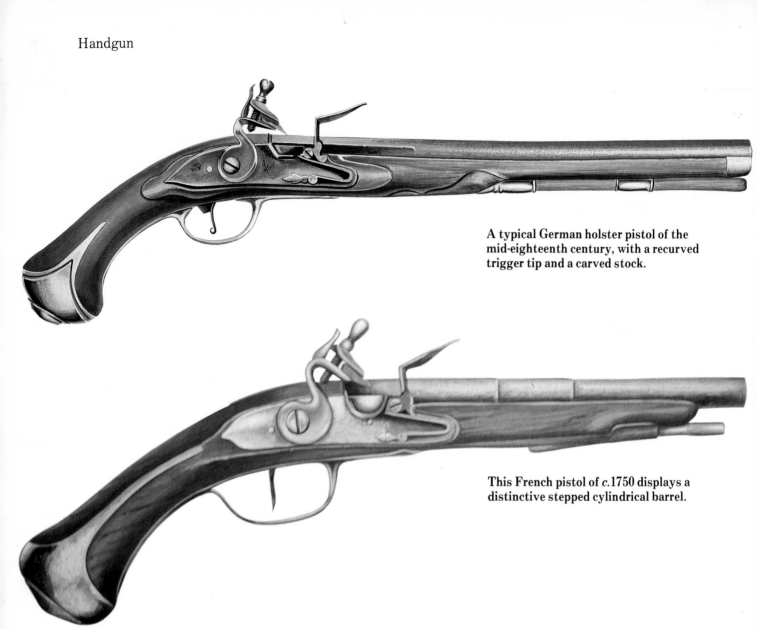

A typical German holster pistol of the mid-eighteenth century, with a recurved trigger tip and a carved stock.

This French pistol of *c.*1750 displays a distinctive stepped cylindrical barrel.

Several improvements in the efficiency of the flintlock occcurred during the late eighteenth century. The so-called 'waterproof pan' arose from deepening and narrowing the pan (presenting less surface to damp), improving the fit of the frizzen over the pan and providing additional drain channels. A roller between the frizzen and its spring improved the smoothness of the action immeasurably, and Henry Nock reduced the delay between the flash in the pan and the ignition of the main propelling charge by means of a short flash-hole and a sub-diameter, pre-ignition chamber. By 1780, therefore, the flintlock had all but reached the limits of its development potential and – apart from refinements such as screwless locks and platinum-lined touch-holes – could go no further.

Unfortunately, none of the various flinted locks gave instantaneous ignition. This was not evident on the battlefield, where armies still fought in regimented lines and a misdirected shot was often just as effective as an accurate one. But the perceptible pause was very obvious when wildfowling; canny birds reputedly veered on the flash of the priming, a sad miss resulting when the

A Scottish flintlock pistol by Thomas Murdoch of Doune, *c.*1770.

The French Mle 1777 ('Charleville') flintlock pistol featured an all-metal frame with a belt hook on the left side.

main charge ignited. This particular problem so occupied a Presbyterian minister, the Reverend Alexander Forsyth of Belhelvie, Aberdeenshire, that he determined to seek a solution in contemporary chemistry. After unsuccessfully developing with a frizzen cover, to hide the flash of ignition, Forsyth began experimenting with the notoriously unstable metallic fulminates discovered by Berthollet and the Englishman Edward Howard between 1775 and 1800.

Painstakingly, Forsyth attempted to ignite mercuric fulminate in the flintlock pan and then by striking it with a modified cock. Neither system improved on the standard flintlock; not until early in 1805 did the enterprising clergyman find a solution by confining a suitable priming powder in a small space and striking it with a special hammer. Considerably encouraged, Forsyth left for London at the request of the Master General of Ordnance.

Unfortunately, a new and much less sympathetic Master General ordered Forsyth from the Tower of London while the lock was being readied for military trials. Undaunted, the inventor approached the

31

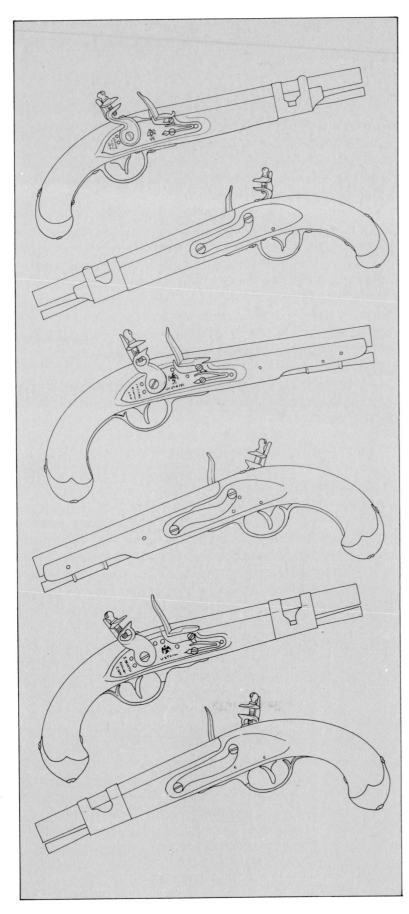

Some U.S. martial flintlocks: (top) the M1807 made by Springfield Armory; middle, a Simeon North-made M1811; and bottom, the M1811 with Wickham's improvement.

More U.S. flintlocks. Top, M1813 and M1816, both made by North; middle, the M1817 made by Springfield Armory; and bottom, the M1819.

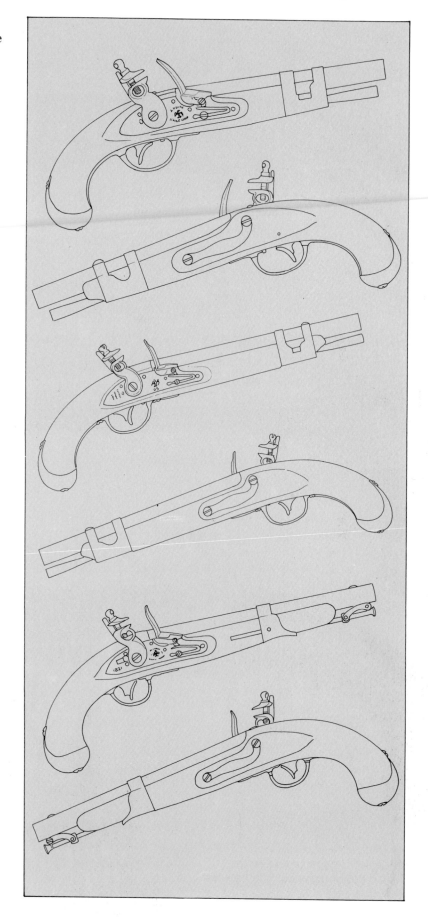

The American Kentucky pistol was as distinctive as the longrifles. This example dates from the late eighteenth century.

Above: A blunderbuss pistol by Clark & Son, London, *c.*1780. The belled muzzle facilitated shot-dispersion.

Below: An English flintlock by Ezekiel Baker, London, *c.*1800. A swivel ramrod often denotes Sea Service.

An eprouvette or powder-tester. The efficacy of the powder was gauged by the rotation of the muzzle-plate against the spring.

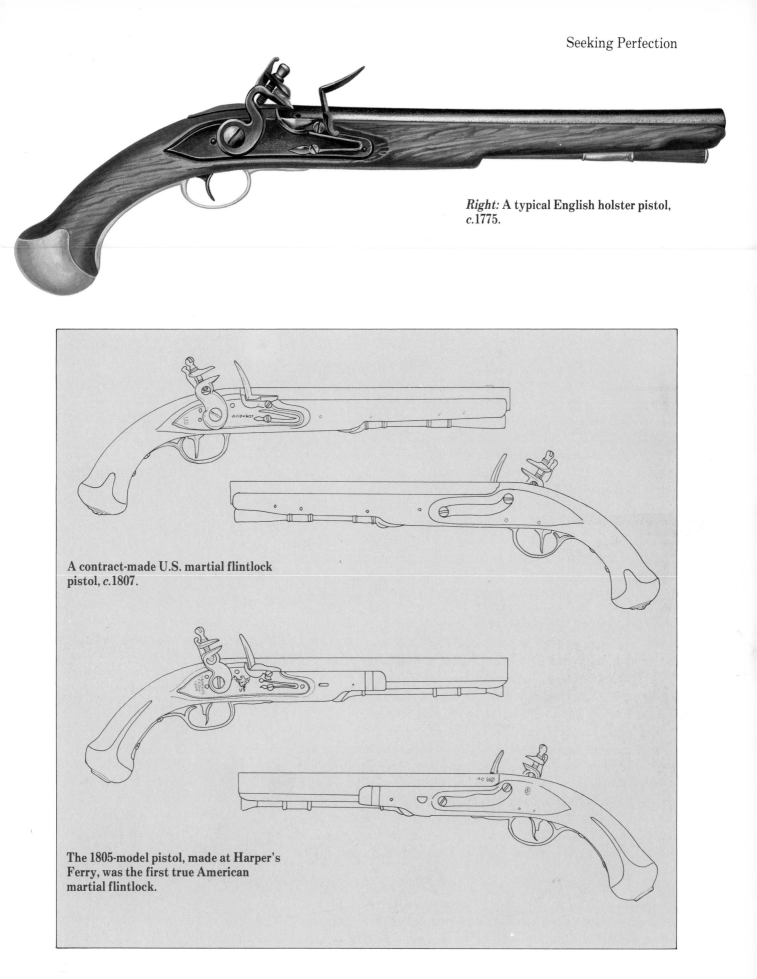

Right: A typical English holster pistol, *c.*1775.

A contract-made U.S. martial flintlock pistol, *c.*1807.

The 1805-model pistol, made at Harper's Ferry, was the first true American martial flintlock.

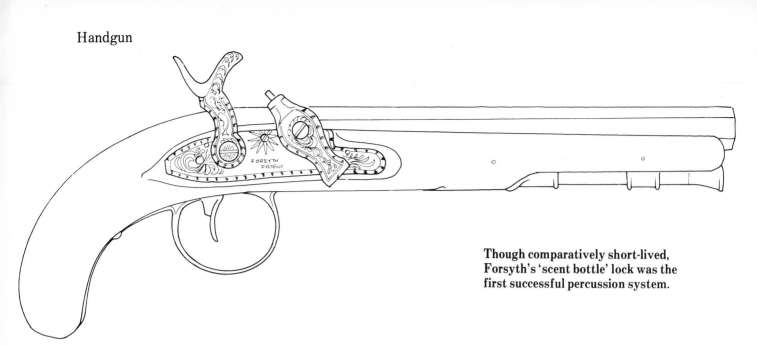

Though comparatively short-lived, Forsyth's 'scent bottle' lock was the first successful percussion system.

engineer James Watt, the lock was perfected, and Patent 3,032/1807 was granted on 17 April 1807 to run for fourteen years. The guns were to be made by John Prosser of 9 Charing Cross, London, but the arrangement was unsatisfactory and production rights soon reverted to the Forsyth Patent Gun Company of No.10 Piccadilly. Forsyth and his cousin, James Brougham, retained an interest in the company until 1819, after which it continued as 'Forsyth & Co., Patent Gunmakers' under the ownership of its former manager. Trading finally ceased in 1852.

The original 'scent bottle' lock consisted of a rotary magazine of priming powder mounted on the outside of a conventional lock-plate, which also supported a specially flat-faced hammer. Once the gun had been muzzle-loaded, the hammer was placed on half-cock and the priming magazine rotated through 180 degrees. This metered a tiny amount of the 'oxymuriate salts' into the flash-hole channel, whereafter the magazine was returned to its original position to effect a seal between the flash-hole and the magazine spindle. The hammer was then drawn back to full cock, the trigger pressed, and the hammer fell onto a small firing pin protruding from the top of the magazine. The blow drove the pin into the flash-hole aperture, detonating the priming and initiating the main charge.

The 'scent bottle' was practically waterproof, gave great certainty of ignition and was clearly an improvement over the flintlocks. However, it was complicated and expensive to make; and the seal between the priming magazine and the magazine spindle became less efficient with wear. As the priming composition proved to be highly corrosive, the mechanism also had to be cleaned after every firing. These factors conspired to restrict the distribution of Forsyth's lock, which cost as much as a normal flintlock sporting gun.

Even during the life of Forsyth's patent, gunsmiths in Britain attempted to improve the potentially world-beating idea. Some of the solutions proved to be flawed; some were downright dangerous; a few worked sufficiently well for their inventor's names to be remembered. Forsyth himself developed a variant of the scent bottle in which a drum rotated on a vertical axis. In other systems, gum arabic, iron oxide or a similar binder was used to mould the fulminate powder into 'pills', which were either placed in the hammer (patented by Joseph Manton in 1816) or inserted in the flash-hole. Joseph Manton in England and the American chemist Samuel Guthrie claimed paternity of a lock in which the priming composition was contained in a soft metal tube, half of which was inserted in the flash-hole while the exposed half was struck by the hammer. Disc-primer systems in which a small circle of primer was held between two pieces of cartridge paper were developed in the U.S.A. by Christian Sharps and Butterfield & Marshall, and applied successfully to rifles and revolvers respectively. The tape primer was similar to the disc system, but the discs were contained in a continuous paper roll; originating in France as early as 1821 (Laboeuf de Valdehon's patent), this was developed by Herteloup and then by the American dentist Edward Maynard. Maynard tape primers were successful enough to persuade the United States government to acquire the rights.

Most of these systems worked as well, if not better, than Forsyth's but were not without disadvantages. The pill-lock primers were vulnerable to knocks in transit, some of the tube locks flew out of the flash-hole when the main charge ignited, and the cartridge-paper disc and tape systems were rarely wholly waterproof. The answer was to be found in the copper cap, in which a small amount of mercuric fulminate or potassium chlorate was contained in what looked like an inverted top-hat. Covered by a thin tinfoil disc and sealed with shellac, this durable and completely watertight product proved an ideal basis for the percussion system.

Small percussion 'travelling pistols' usually had folding triggers. This example was sold by Colgan of Limerick about 1845.

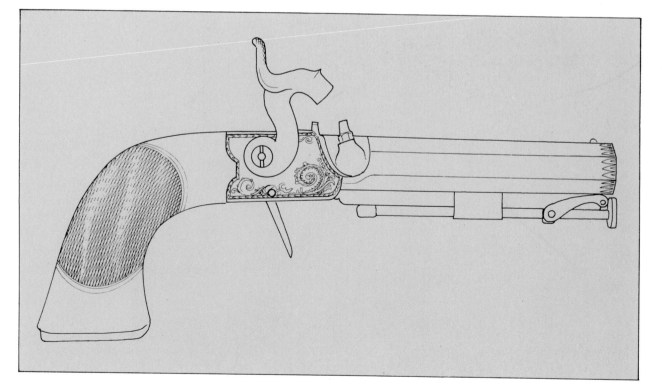

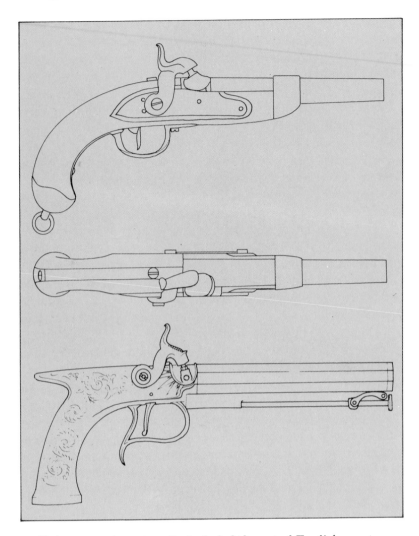

A typical Belgian percussion-ignition
military pistol, 1830.

An English all-metal saw-handled
percussion pistol of *c.*1840.

Claimants to its paternity included the noted English sportsman
Peter Hawker; gunsmiths Joseph Egg and James Purdey; and E.
Goode Wright, whose papers published in *The Philosophical
Magazine and Journal* in 1823 were largely responsible for
promoting the cap at a time when the pill- and tube-locks were most
widely distributed. Purdey had been associated with Forsyth during
the perfection of the scent bottle lock and maintained that he had
made the first cap from an umbrella tag! The earliest patent can be
disregarded, as it was granted in France on 28 July 1820 to the
gunmaker Prélat – a notorious copyist – and is unlikely to have
been original.

A more plausible claimant is an English-born artist, Joshua Shaw,
who is believed to have made the first iron cap in 1814 or 1815 and
had graduated to pewter and then copper by 1816. However, the
manner of Shaw's discovery may be argued (his own colourful story
is most probably apocryphal) and he emigrated to America in 1817
without applying for a patent. Shaw later claimed that he doubted
whether his invention would be permissible, as Forsyth's patent
remained enforceable until 1821; and as an alien, he had to wait a
minimum of two years before applying for a U.S. Patent. Though
this was not granted until June 1822, the destruction of the U.S.

A Russian percussion pistol from the
mid-nineteenth century.

H. HOLLAND,
Manufacturer of
GUNS, RIFLES, PISTOLS,
and every description of
BREECH LOADING
AND REVOLVING CHAMBERED FIRE ARMS,
98, New Bond Street, LONDON. W.

This trade card was used by Harris Holland, who began trading in London in 1850 and later founded the well known gunsmith Holland & Holland.

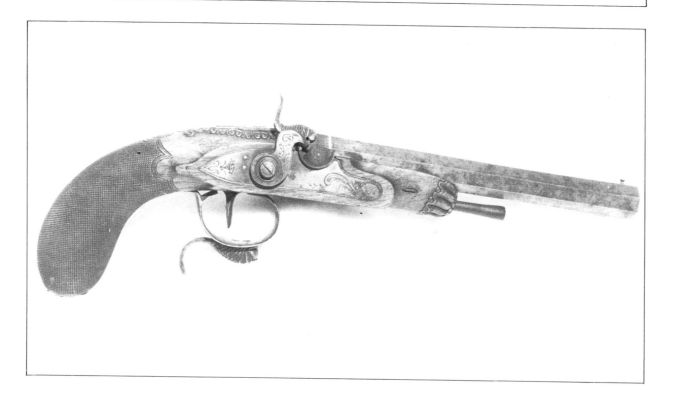

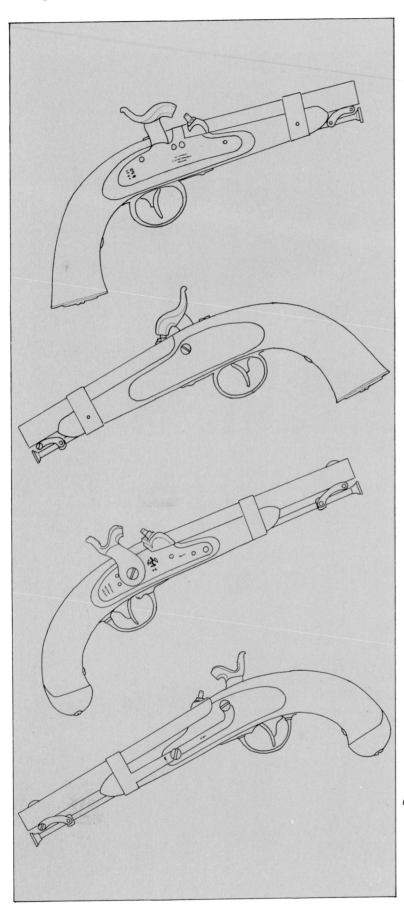

More U.S. martial pistols. Top, the M1842 with an internal hammer; middle, a variant with a conventional external hammer; and, bottom, the U.S. Pistol-Carbine M1855.

The Forsyth lock with the magazine in the priming position (top) and ready to fire (bottom).

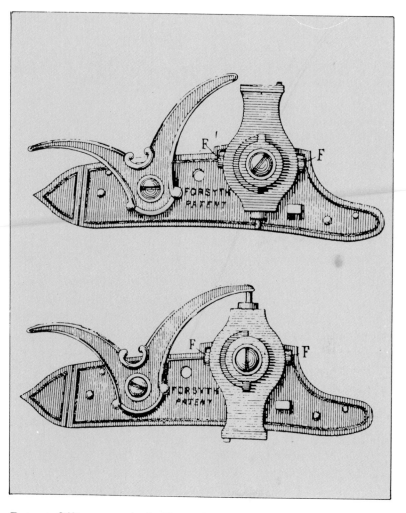

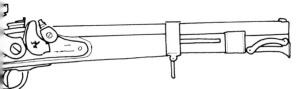

Patent Office records in December 1836 has now obscured the progress of Shaw's applications.

Devotees of the percussion cap claimed that their system ignited more certainly than their flintlock rivals, which was undoubtedly true, and also that there was less of a delay between pulling the trigger and discharging the bullet. Flintlock *aficionados* countered that theirs was the 'stronger shooting' method, the claim, they said, being borne out by tests undertaken by the British Army showing that flintlocks often generated greater muzzle velocity than comparably-loaded percussion-ignition guns.

The percussion system ultimately prevailed because it was easier to use and – most importantly – easier to teach. It provided the basis for the pepperboxes and revolvers of the mid-nineteenth century, and had a profound effect on the progress of shooting. The irony was that Alexander Forsyth, who had achieved so much to change the course of firearms history, should have received so little reward; in 1840, after much petitioning, he was awarded the trifling sum of £200 by the British Government and, after his death in 1842, a public outcry pricked the conscience of the authorities into granting a further £1,000 to Forsyth's heirs. This makes an interesting comparison with the fortunes of Colt, whose success would have been nothing without Forsyth's original invention.

3. Change for Change's Sake

A rare invention to Destroy the Crowd
Of Fools at Home instead of Foes Abroad,
Fear not my Friends, this Terrible Machine;
They're only Wounded that have Shares therein.

The Bubbler's Mirrour, or England's Folley lampooning the Puckle
Gun, *c.*1719

Though most men have been satisfied with conventional firearms
throughout history, a few independently-minded souls have always
demanded something different. The object of their endeavours has
almost always been to improve power or rapidity of fire and though
some of their ideas have fared better than others, few lack interest.

Breech-loading and multi-barrel systems may be encountered in
even the earliest firearms. The commonest form of breech-loader
had a conventionally hooped iron barrel set into a wrought-iron
frame containing a cylindrical chamber. Once the gun had been
fired, the wedge retaining the breech chamber was knocked out, a
fresh chamber substituted for the spent one, the wedge replaced
and the gun fired again. Though manufacturing standards were
poor, barrels and breech-chambers burst regularly, and the chamber
and barrel generally sealed badly, these guns still held considerable
promise. But though removable-chamber matchlocks were made –
a carbine and a much altered pistol made for Henry VIII survive in
the Tower of London – the problems of sealing the breech defeated
experimenters until the advent of the self-contained metallic
cartridge.

Excepting the revolving cylinder and its near relation, the
revolving barrel-cluster, the most popular of the early multi-shot
systems consisted simply of loading powder charges, bullets and
wads alternately into a single barrel, and then using either multiple
or sliding locks to fire each charge sequentially. Unfortunately,
unless the wads sealed the system properly, these guns had an
unpleasant habit of firing all the shots in an elongated volley;
excessive pressure then sometimes wrecked the gun and maimed or
even killed the firer.

Illustrations of Klotzbüchsen, containing alternate charges of
powder and iron or leaden balls (Klotzen), appear in a manuscript in
the Stadtsbibliothek, Vienna, dating from the first half of the
fifteenth century; and a similar multi-charge gun is described in a
German 'Feuerwehrbuch', printed in 1529 but based on manuscript
sources extending back to 1420. More recent examples include a
Russian sporting gun displaying four complete French Locks on a
single lock-plate, accessing each in turn by a sliding trigger block;

The 'Damascus' barrel was made by twisting iron bars around a mandrel, hammer-welding the joints and then etching the surface to bring out the characteristic decorative patterning.

Hinged- or scissors-type moulds were the easiest means of casting bullets prior to the advent of the metallic cartridge.

and the Anglo-American Jover & Belton sliding lock, a few of which were made in London for the East India Company (1785-88) before it was discovered that the detachable seven-shot loading chamber infringed an earlier patent. French Lock longarms were also made on the Chambers system (twelve shot, fixed barrel, multiple lock); by the American gunsmith Simeon North (ten shot, fixed barrel, sliding lock); and by Henry W. Mortimer of London, whose four-shot rifle was similar to North's. These were succeeded by percussion-ignition guns made by William Mills of London on the Ritso System, with a sliding lock and four caps, and by the French Ramel System, with a four-shot metal cartridge. August Robert patented a series of percussion-cap underhammers in 1839, and Gardon, Aubry & Robert then replaced Robert's sliding actuator with a helical clock spring.

The Bechtler 'double-end' pistol of 1850 had two barrels, one of which served as the grip.

The most successful superimposed-charge guns were the American Walch and Lindsay patterns, though clearly owing something to 1827-vintage French ideas. The revolver patented by Walch in February 1859 relied on a single barrel and an elongated cylinder in which each chamber held two charges. The .36 calibre six-chamber twelve-shot and the .31 calibre five-chamber ten-shot relied on twin hammers to fire in the correct order, but were prone to fire both loads at once. The original .36 guns had twin triggers, but most of the later .31 pattern incorporated a single trigger patented by John Lindsay in October 1860. Production guns were made for the J.P. Lindsay Manufacturing Company.

The Lindsay rifle-musket externally resembled an M1855 Springfield, but with two hammers actuated by a single trigger. The trigger fired the front charge first, the cap-flame passing through an extended flash-hole bored in the barrel-side; and even if the rear-charge hammer was cocked and fired alone, the gun was still strong enough to take the resulting two-shot volley. A thousand Lindsay muskets were ordered in 1863, and at least one Indian band paid the penalty for rashly assuming that the soldiers were reloading after the first volley. A few single-barrelled two-shot 'Young America' pistols embodying the same system were also made in the early 1860s.

The Walch revolver inspired a series of multi-cylinder and double-barrel revolvers. Charles Sneider's patent of March 1862 protected two cylinders back-to-back, while George Gardner's gun of May 1865 had two cylinders in tandem, a bored-through chamber allowing shots from the second cylinder to pass through the first into the barrel. The most incredible was William Phillips' 1873-vintage design which had three seven-chamber cylinders containing seventeen shots (6 + 5 + 6), and automatically rotated a new cylinder into position once the preceding one had been expended. The twin-barrel guns included an 18-shot .22 rimfire example patented by

An English seven-barrel volley pistol of about 1785.

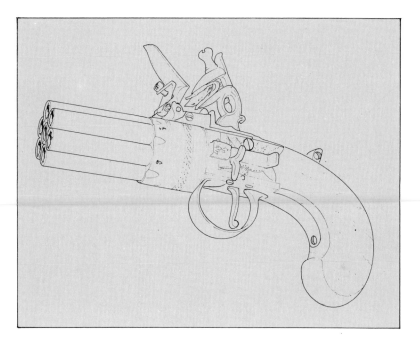

Below: A pair of Swiss six-barrelled volley pistols.

An English Brasher six-barrel flintlock, with a tap mechanism on the barrel block.

Albert Christ of California, Ohio, in September 1866; a rotatable-barrel Owen Jones design of June 1874, whose spare cylinder was stowed in the butt; and Freeman Hood's 'Osgood Duplex' of December 1880, somewhat like the Le Mat described in Chapter 4, which offered eight .22 rimfire cartridges in the cylinder and a single .32 rimfire shot from the central barrel.

Comparatively few superimposed-load systems were applied to pistols, as they were appreciably longer than multiple-barrel systems of comparable capacity. However, surviving examples include a twin-barrel/four-shot Dutch Lock holster pistol with selectable flash-holes; or a seven-shot with a sliding French Lock and a removable loading chamber controlled by tipping the barrel downward. The twin-barrel gun has split lock-plates, with a single cock on the breech and duplicated steels or frizzens on the barrels. However, sealing multiple flash-holes by sliding catches or pivoting lids promoted chain-firing, which partly explains their rarity compared with conventional (but otherwise comparable) multi-barrelled guns.

As the dangers of superimposing loads were soon established, an aggregation of single-shot barrels seemed preferable. The most

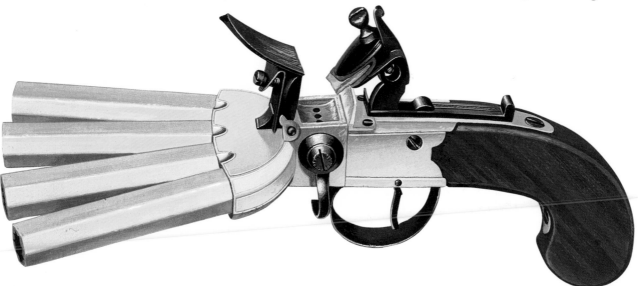

These pistols were named for the resemblance their cluster of splayed barrels bore to a duck's foot. The barrels fired simultaneously.

popular method was originally to group several barrels together around a central axis, retaining them with iron hoops, and then ignite each barrel in turn with a lighted coal or a slow-match. This method retained its popularity in some of the more primitive areas of the Far East well into the eighteenth century, along with a variant with its barrels secured horizontally in a flattened cage. Primitive cluster barrels subsequently developed into guns with their barrels in a fixed block, the revolving-barrel gun, and indirectly to the revolver. The weight of multiple barrels restricted them to carbines or, more commonly, pistols.

Two or more fixed barrels, ignited in a volley from a single lock or independently by separate locks, were preferred to revolving-barrel wheel-locks, but the advent of flinted locks enabled the cock to be

Two-barrel flintlocks made by Thomas Galton of London, c.1786.

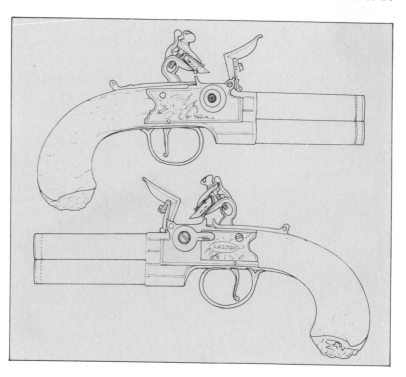

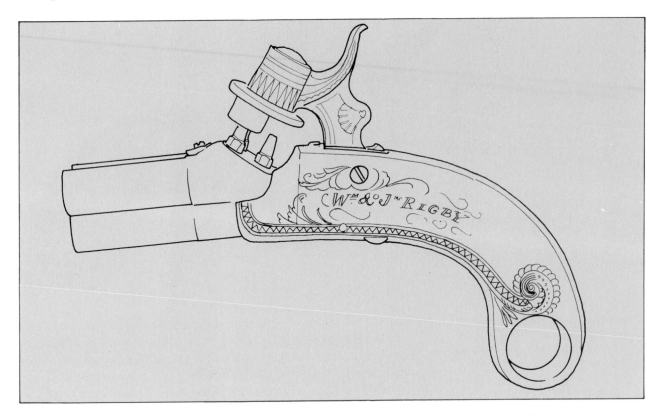

A three-barrel pistol by Rigby, Dublin, c.1835.

split from the steel with greater ease. The earliest representatives include two-barrel 'over and under' guns with either left- and right-hand locks or one cock/two frizzen systems; three- and four-barrel guns with one cock/several-frizzen Dutch or French Locks, made in every conceivable size from pocket to holster pistol; and others, much more rarely encountered, with clusters of as many as seven barrels. Owing to the increasing weight, however, pre-pepperbox guns with six or more barrels usually feature block construction.

Fixed-block multi-barrel systems were particularly popular in England when allied with box-lock construction and a central cock. Though many relied on the volley to make up for deficiencies of calibre or aim, some featured a radial selector on the side of the barrel block. Several shots could then be fired, though each required a separate priming action and movement of the selector. The multi-barrel block was long lived, examples being the 3-barrel Marston pistol with a selectable striker, patented in May 1857 and improved in 1864; a four-barrel pocket pistol patented by Christian Sharps in 1859 and made under licence in Britain by Tipping & Lawden; the German Reform, Regnum, Tomma and Bär pistols; the British 1881-patent Lancaster Howdah Pistol and the Braendlin 'Mitrailleuse Pistol', made in calibres as large as .476; and, of course, the renowned Remington double-barrel deringer. Of these, all but the Reform group and the Bär used fixed barrels or barrel-blocks and hammer/trigger systems that fired each barrel in sequence. The barrel block of the Reform moved vertically each time the trigger was pulled, firing one barrel at a time from a constant hammer position, while the Bär used a combination of double barrels, a sequencing firing system and a pivoting breechblock.

The oddest of the 'barrel block' guns was the later metallic-cartridge Jarré Harmonica pistol, patented in France in 1873, in which the whole barrel block moved one place laterally each time the hammer was cocked. This was adapted from the earlier fixed-barrel sliding breechblock Jarre pinfire gun, patented in 1862, but the principle was much the same. Unfortunately, unlike the Reform, whose barrel-block travelled vertically, the lateral movement of the Jarré system upset the balance appreciably.

Neither the rotary barrel cluster nor a barrel-block, whether static or mobile, was ideal in a pistol in which economy of weight and size was always desirable. The best compromise would clearly be a single-barrelled gun either with multiple breech-chambers – the revolver – or some kind of magazine. The earliest magazine systems were extraordinary *tours de force* for their time, and inventors such as the Dane Kalthoff, whose work dated from the middle of the seventeenth century, deserved much more success than the limitations of gunpowder would allow.

The Kalthoff system was never applied to a magazine pistol, the most interesting early representative of which is credited to the Florentine gunmaker Michele Lorenzoni – even though copies were made by Domenico Berselli of Bologna and John Cookson of London. Several similar guns were made by William Grice of

The four-barrel Lancaster pistol, patented by H.A.A. Thorn in 1881, chambered cartridges as large as .476.

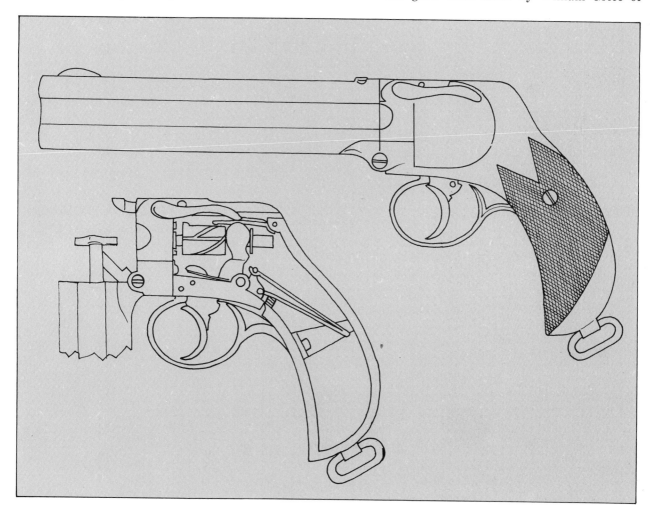

London in the 1770s, and others by Henry Mortimer in 1795-8.

Berselli's variant of the Lorenzoni system consists of a vertical disc-type breechblock with two holes bored into its periphery. A ball tube and a powder magazine run up through the butt to the breech-disc housing. Once the gun has been fired, an operating handle on the left side is rotated forward and, provided the muzzle is pointed downward, a ball rolls forward from the magazine tube into the shallower of the breech-disc recesses while the longer of the two fills with powder. As the lever is returned to its original position, the ball rolls out of the breech-disc aperture into the barrel; and, as the operating handle comes to the end of its travel, the ball aperture is rotated down past the barrel and is replaced by the powder chamber. Here the mechanism comes to rest, with the powder chamber and barrel in near-perfect alignment, and the flash-hole bored obliquely through the breech-disc aligning with the pan.

The Lorenzoni system worked well enough in theory, but was beset with several practical problems. However well made the guns may have been, the flash of ignition sometimes crept around the periphery of the breech-disc to ignite the powder magazine. Thus, despite the skill with which the whole system was conceived, it was always destined to fail.

Attempts were still being made to devise an efficient powder-and-ball repeater as late as 1840, when Orville Percival of Moodus, Connecticut, developed a barrel sleeve which, carrying the powder and ball containers as well as priming, could be reloaded merely by rotating it through 180 degrees. The obsolescent design was not patented by Percival & Smith until 1850; the 'Smith' was in fact Horace Smith, later to be a founding partner of Smith & Wesson.

If success eluded the earliest magazine systems, the single-shot breechloaders promised much more. These included a plug-type breech actuated by the trigger guard, patented by Isaac de la Chaumette in 1714, and the later (but somewhat similar) British Ferguson. The principle was simply that a rapid-pitch thread, when

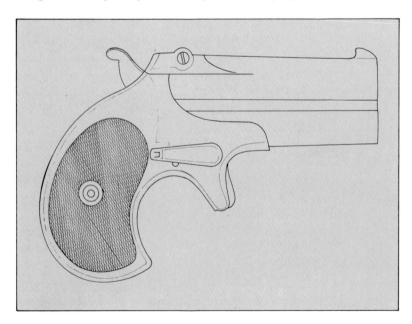

Patented by William Eliott in 1865, the popular Remington deringer remained in production until 1935.

This pinfire Jarré Harmonica Gun, patented in 1862, had a unique laterally-moving magazine block.

Prior to the appearance of the Jarré pistol, percussion 'harmonica' guns were made in small numbers.

turned by a separate spanner or the trigger-guard, dropped the plug to give access to the breech. This could then be loaded with a tight-fitting ball, wadding and a suitable powder charge, and the plug wound back to seal the breech. The system proved effectual, but needed to be well made if no gas was to escape from the plug-way. Though most surviving guns are longarms, one or two Ferguson-type pistols are known.

A more popular variation on the theme was the 'turn-off' barrel, dating back to the first quarter of the seventeenth century. The guns – which usually embodied French Locks though alternatives are known – have an unsupported cannon-type barrel screwed to the standing breech. A special spanner can be inserted in the muzzle and the barrel turned until it comes away from the gun. A ball, wadding and powder charge are then inserted in a breech chamber, and the barrel is replaced on the frame. Though the screw thread could be damaged, preventing efficient operation, the turn-off barrel guns were sturdy and could accept tight-fitting balls to improve accuracy. The oft-repeated story of how in 1642 the Royalist Prince Rupert twice pierced the weather-cock on St Mary's Church, Stafford, with successive shots from a rifled turn-off barrel pistol at more than 60 yards, would have been stretching credulity with a contemporary smoothbore Dog Lock!

Turn-off barrel guns enjoyed more than a century in vogue, and are now often labelled as 'cannon barrelled' or 'Queen Anne', even though most were made long after the queen's brief reign in 1702-14.

Single-shot breechloading pistols enjoyed considerable vogue in the nineteenth century, particularly once the first steps had been taken towards metallic cartridges. The most enterprising of the earliest inventors was the Swiss Samuel Johann Pauly, who spent much of his time working in Paris and London. In 1812, Pauly received a French patent for a breech-loading gun in which the barrel hinged down to allow the insertion of a special thick-base metal cartridge. Settling in Britain after the fall of Paris, he patented an improvement in which a small spring-piston system compressed air so rapidly that it became hot enough to ignite the propellant even after passing through the hollow flash-tube in the

Above: **A typical English turn-off barrel or 'Queen Anne' pistol, *c.*1740.**

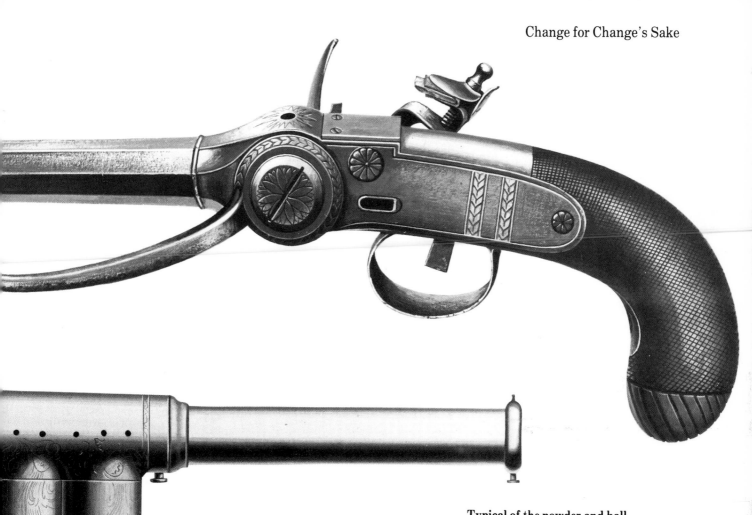

Typical of the powder-and-ball
breechloaders were those of Domenico
Berselli (Lorenzoni system, *top*) and the
1850-patent Percival & Smith magazine
pistol (*left*).

Below: A typical English turn-off barrel
pistol marked 'Cornhill, London', *c.*1760.

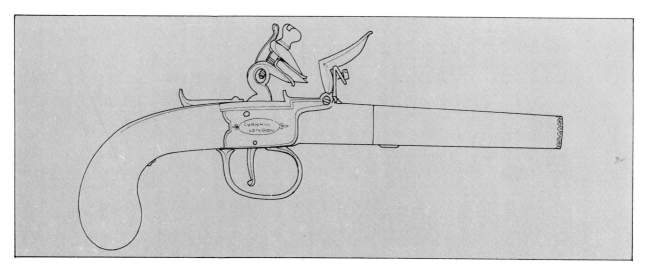

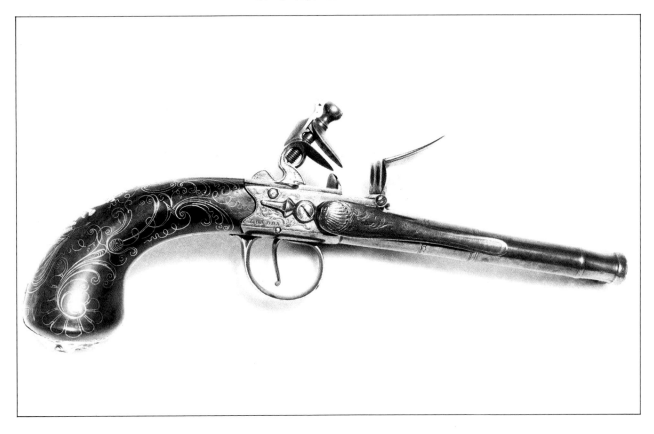

Above: **Some Pauly breechloaders featured air ignition, but many, such as this Manton-made example, were converted to use conventional percussion caps.**

cartridge base. Some air-ignition guns were made in London by John Manton, though their period in vogue was short. Pauly's successors reverted to a percussion cap and an internal striker.

During this period, the French were particularly active; early self-contained cartridges included the centre-fire Galy-Cazalat pattern of 1826, Casimir Lefaucheux's first crude pinfire (1828), Pottet's centre-fire metal-based paper cartridge of 1829, and the rimfire Robert of 1831. The unsuccessful French Robert pistol of 1832 had a fixed barrel and a radial breechblock, operated by a lever running down the back of the grip, but the cartridge was still too flimsy to ensure certain ignition and gas often leaked fom the breech.

In Prussia, Johann Niklaus Dreyse, once apprenticed to Pauly, made the first of his needle-fire pistols in association with Kaufmann Collenbusch. However, unlike his better-known rifles, these muzzle-loaders had a crank-cocked spring-loaded igniting needle in the rear of the action. The later Dreyse breech-loading pistols incorporated either a military-style bolt action or a variant of Dreyse's needle-fire sporting mechanism, in which a radial underlever cammed the barrel out for loading while cocking the firing needle. None, however, encountered much success.

Contemporary with Dreyse bolt-action pistols were the American dropping-block patterns made to the patents of Christian Sharps (1848-59), William Marston (1850) and Alonzo Perry (1855), which proved to be strong and effectual if not altogether gas-tight. In the same era, the Frenchmen Lefaucheux and Houllier produced a collection of metallic cartridges, and their countrymen Devisme and Flobert began to produce the first of many low-powered target or saloon pistols. The Flobert-Regnier system relied on cartridges in which the minimal power derived solely from a small charge of fulminate, and a powerful spring-propelled hammer block provided sufficient of a breech-lock in most Flobert pistols.

Altogether different were the powerful single-shot metallic cartridge pistols such as the Remington Rolling Blocks, several models of which were purchased by the U.S. Navy in 1865-72; a host of Stevens guns with tipping barrels; and a number of specialised single-shot target pistols whose influence, both in the United States and in Europe, remains considerable. The best known of these have been the Smith & Wessons, several patterns of which were built on revolveresque lines from 1893 until the introduction of the perfected 'Straight Line' in 1925, and the Colt Camp Perry Model (1926-39). The most effectual of the pre-1939 designs, however, are the German-made modified Aydt or Martini system dropping-block designs typified by the sophisticated Luna and Tell target pistols.

Attempts have often been made to develop combination weapons in which, for example, a pistol could be combined with a sword or mace. This concept had a lengthy pedigree, traceable back to the 'Holy Water Sprinklers' of the sixteenth century, which combined

Below and left: **A pistol by Barber, London, c.1765.**

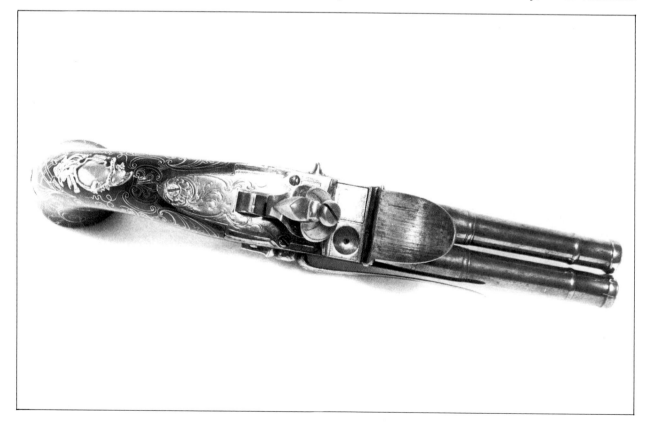

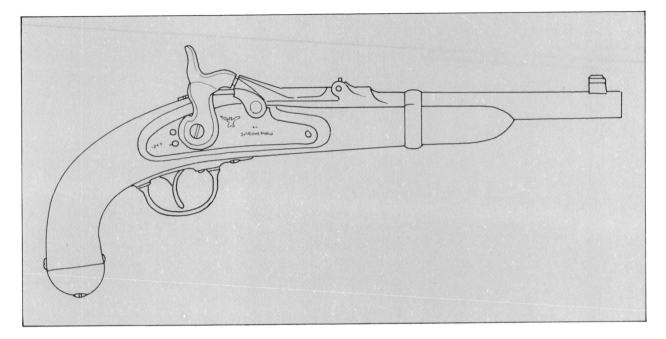

several firelock or matchlock barrels with a spear blade and, more often than not, a halo or two of spikes. Then came combination wheel-lock pistols and battle-axes or war hammers, pistol-lances, extraordinary hybrid halberd-pistol-forks, and on into flintlock pistols – originating from Iberia to the Caucasus – in which the butt terminates in a massive ball. This idea persisted into the present century, Robert Gordon-Smith patenting a dagger-butt for revolvers as late as 1897.

By the nineteenth century, the projects had become more sophisticated and included a single-barrel pistol-sword, incorporating a Birmingham-made percussion pistol, credited to the London sword-cutler Joshua Johnson about 1800. The most notorious is the Pistol-Cutlass patented by George Elgin in 1837. This combination of a single-shot percussion-ignition pistol and a

Above: The single-shot U.S. Pistol M1869, with Allin's 'trapdoor' breech.

The breech mechanism of Mauser's C/76 single-shot pistol was carried on an arm extending beneath the barrel.

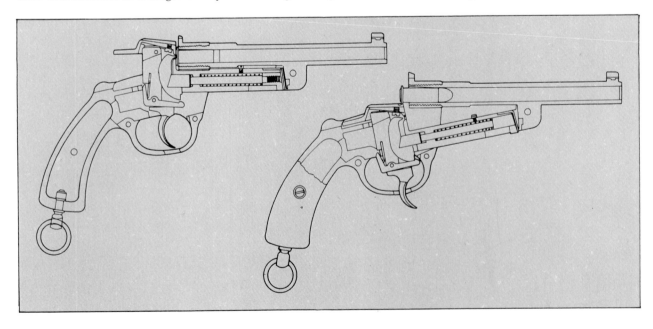

The Remington M1871 Rolling Block pistol, though one of the finest of its type, was doomed by the perfection of the revolver.

The 'No.2' Deringer was made by the National Arms Company until the operations were acquired by Colt in 1870.

short heavy chopping blade was acquired by the U.S. Navy for the South Seas Exploring Expedition (1838-9), but when the expedition returned, the manufacturers – C.B. Allen of Springfield and Merrill, Mosman & Blair of Amherst, Massachusetts – had both gone into liquidation.

Elgin's experiences did not deter other hopeful inventors, and inspired a rash of weapons such as Robert Andrews' pistol-sword and Robert Lawton's sabre-sword, both of which were patented in 1837. Interest in combination weapons predictably revived during the U.S. Civil War, during which Robert Colvin Jun. patented a six-shot cavalry sabre in March 1862 and James Campbell contributed a pistol-lance (June 1863). Another favourite from this period was the pistol-knife made by the Sheffield cutlery manufacturers Unwin & Rodgers or its affiliate, James Rodgers; the earliest examples

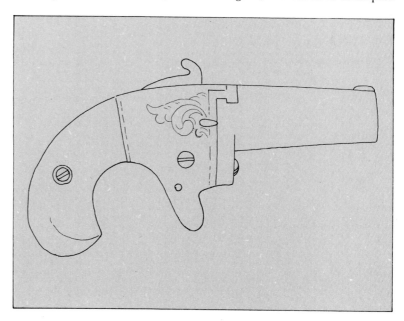

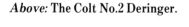

Above: **The Colt No.2 Deringer.**

A flintlock pistol-knife and pistol-fork, made in southern Germany by 'WM' in the eighteenth century.

featured percussion ignition, but later pin- or rimfire versions are known.

While the single-shot percussion-ignition breechloader was encountering limited success, many inventors returned to the problems of increasing the fire-rate and the perfection of the mechanically-operated revolver by Samuel Colt (see Chapter 4). These short cluster-barrel guns were simpler than the first Paterson Colts and easier to make. Shortly after Colt had received his first U.S. Patent, a pepperbox was patented by the brothers Benjamin and Barton Darling; as the barrel-clusters of the guns pictured in the patent are rotated mechanically, it has even been claimed (somewhat unrealistically) that the Darling brothers pre-empted Colt.

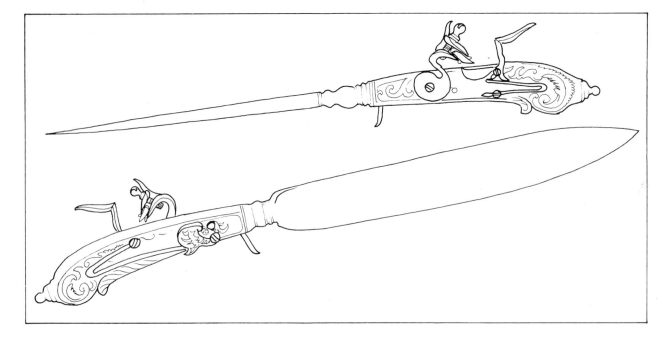

The Darling pepperbox was made in painfully small numbers by several different contractors. Many guns lack mechanical rotation and the Darling was less important than the contemporary double-action manual-rotation pepperbox patented by Ethan Allen. This outsold the Paterson Colts appreciably in the period 1837-45, largely because of its rapidity of fire. However, Allen's bar hammer rose through the sight line and hindered deliberate shooting. Like most of its immediate contemporaries, too, the Allen pepperbox was also prone to chain-firing – though this was less serious in a cluster-barrel gun than in a revolver, where one or more of the unexpected shots would strike the frame.

The Darling and Allen pepperboxes were but two American representatives of a very popular class. Many percussion examples were made in Britain, while the later Continental European examples were often pinfire. Among the most popular brands were the 'Mariettes', a generic term for a ring-trigger pepperbox of Belgian, French or even English origin; 'My Friend', a small pepperbox/knuckleduster patented by James Reid of Catskill, New York, in December 1865; and the later Dolne 'Apache' – named after the Parisian roughnecks – which was amalgamated with knuckledusters and a folding bayonet. Delahaxhe made a similar multi-purpose gun, and the idea was revived in Britain during World War II. The pepperbox lost favour after the expiry of the Colt patent in 1855 allowing a flood of percussion revolvers onto the market, and though the pinfires were being marketed well into the 1880s – sometimes as late as the end of the nineteenth century – the cheap rimfire revolver ultimately overcame them as well.

Pepperboxes and percussion revolvers enjoyed 30 years of continuous success and were only relegated to obscurity by the perfection of the metallic cartridge. Turret guns and chain repeaters presented the other side of the coin; with the benefit of hindsight, there seems no good reason for their existence.

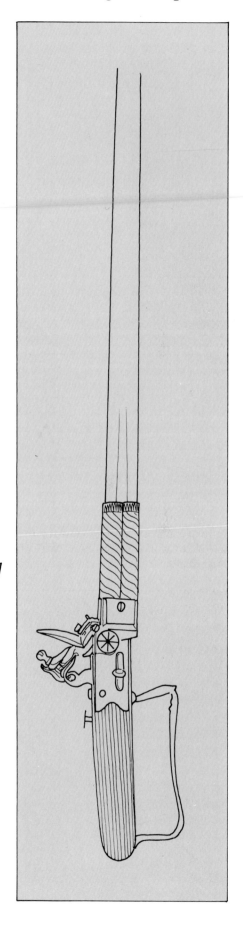

Above: A 'small' Elgin cutlass pistol, made by Merrill, Mosman & Blair of Amherst, Massachusetts, *c.*1837-8.

Right: A multi-barrel flintlock pistol-sword.

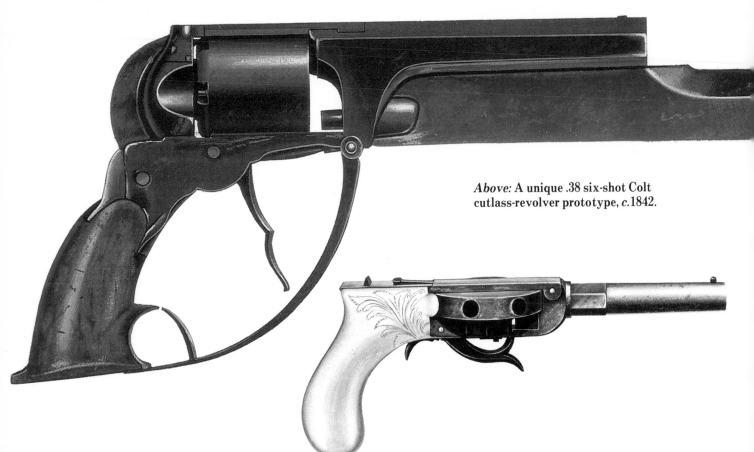

Above: A unique .38 six-shot Colt cutlass-revolver prototype, *c.*1842.

Above, right: A Cochran Monitor turret pistol, *c.*1838.

One of the earliest turret guns was patented by John Webster Cochran in 1837, its horizontal breech-disc containing several peripheral chambers for powder and ball. An underhammer percussion-cap system provided ignition – except when the caps occasionally fell off the nipples as the hammer was thumbed back. A few Cochran 'Monitors' were even made by Wilkinson & Son of London in 1839-41, but the design was as prone to the chain firing phenomenon as the contemporary percussion revolvers. If a revolver or pepperbox chain-fired, the worst that could be expected was a volley rather than a single shot, and an empty gun. Some damage could be done to a revolver frame, it is true; but in the Monitor and other guns of its type, chambers faced outward at the moment of firing and one even faced the firer. Notwithstanding the interposition of the frame and grip, this was potentially very unsafe.

But where Cochran led, many others followed; they included Iverson's twelve-shot percussion pattern, with a mechanically actuated horizontal breech-disc patented in March 1850; Patrick Porter's 'magazine gun', patented in July 1851, which originally amalgamated a vertical disc with an extraordinarily dangerous cylindrical ball/powder magazine on top of the action; Wendell Wright's eight-shot pill lock gun of November 1854, with a vertical disc; Heinrich Genhart's patent of January 1857, in which a combination of a horizontal eight- or ten-shot disc and a lever-operated sliding barrel was claimed to improve the breech-seal; and the French Noël & Guéry pattern, which had an eight-shot vertical

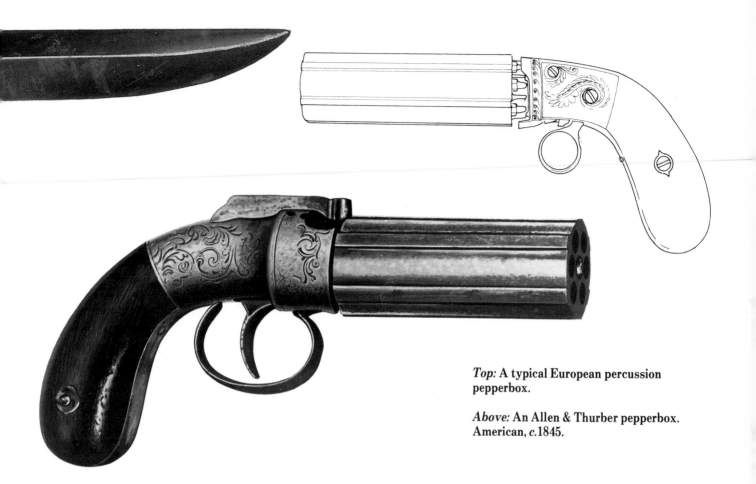

Top: **A typical European percussion pepperbox.**

Above: **An Allen & Thurber pepperbox. American, c.1845.**

disc. A rifle of Porter's design illustrated the worst possible consequences of turret guns by exploding in the inventor's face during a U.S. Army trial in the mid 1850s, fatally wounding him. The turret gun remained more popular with inventors than with the shooting fraternity. The exception was the Turbiaux 'Protector' of 1883, which is considered as a mechanical repeater (see Chapter 6) rather than a turret gun.

Closely allied to the turret-style repeater were guns with an endless belt of cartridge-chambers rotating around the breech as the gun was operated. These offered most of the disadvantages of the turret gun together with greater complexity and weaker construction. The British Treeby Chain Gun was made only as a longarm, but the pistols included the French Gay & Guénot and an American design by Epenetus Bennet and Frederick Haviland of Waterville, Maine (February 1838). Only two of the latter are known, but the Gay & Guénot pistol was offered commercially for some years. A later U.S. patent granted to Henry S. Josselyn in January 1866 protected a chain-revolver whose skeletal cylinder indexed an endless twenty-shot chain. Originally intended for percussion-ignition, the Josselyn (not to be confused with the Joslyn revolver) was later unsuccessfully adapted to rimfire cartridges.

4. Enter the Colonel

They are made of the best steel that can be procured for money, and have the strength to resist the explosive force of gunpowder, while the mongrel imitations and cheap arms are clumsily made of cast iron or inferior materials, and are more dangerous to their owners than they are to all others . . .

from a Colt's Patent Fire Arms Manufacturing Company broadsheet, 1858

Modern handgun history begins with Samuel Colt: though a celebrated explanation of his inspiration – 'from the spokes of a riverboat wheel' – is nothing but hokum, he was undoubtedly the first to market mechanically-actuated revolvers in quantity.

Samuel Colt came from a comparatively wealthy middle-class family. His father, Christopher Colt, owned a silk mill in Hartford, Connecticut, but his mother died when young Samuel was just six years old. After attending preparatory school and Amherst Academy, he then went to sea on the brig *Corvo*, travelling to England and India by the Cape of Good Hope in 1830-31.

During this period, so his first biographer claimed, Colt took the first steps to perfect his revolver. This is probably fanciful legend: having been brought up in the principal gunmaking centre of the United States, Colt probably already knew of the revolving-barrel rifle invented by Artemus Wheeler of Boston (to whom a patent had been granted in June 1818) or the revolving-cylinder guns of Wheeler's protégé, Elisha Collier.

The famous Collier flintlock revolver. Only the earliest featured mechanical cylinder rotation, later guns being manually indexed.

**Prototype Colt revolver No.1, made by
John Pearson of Baltimore about 1834.**

Colt's first experiments date from 1831-2, after the inventor had
successfully hawked patent medicines (as 'Doctor Coult of Calcutta')
to raise finance. The first prototype longarms were made in
Hartford in 1832 by Anson Chase and his assistant, William Rowe,
and showed such promise that improved models had been
commissioned from a Baltimorean mechanic named John Pearson in
1834-5. Colt then approached the authorities in Britain and France;
British Patent 6909 was granted on 22 October 1835, to be followed
by comparable U.S. No.136 on 25 January 1836. Each claimed
advantages such as ease of loading, resistance to damp, the
provision of fences between the cap-nipples to prevent the flash
from one igniting its neighbour, increased rapidity of fire by
connecting the hammer and cylinder-rotating pawl, and the removal
of disturbance of aim as the hammer struck the end (rather than the
top surface) of the cylinder.

Nowhere did Colt, rarely given to modesty, claim to have created
the first revolver with an auto-rotated cylinder. Yet his patent
proved an unyielding barrier to his many rivals, its principal
strength being the claim for hammer-actuated cylinder rotation.
This alone forced designers to circumvent the provision at the
expense of complexity, or to surrender altogether.

In 1835 Colt founded the Patent Arms Manufacturing Company in
Paterson, New Jersey, to exploit his design. He was just 21 years
old. The first guns were revolver-rifles – rejected by the U.S.
Army in 1837 – but Colt then managed to sell fifty rifles and fifty
revolvers to Colonel William Harney of the 2nd Dragoons, serving in
Florida during the Seminole Wars; so obvious was the publicity
value that Colt personally accompanied the shipment to Fort
Jupiter in the winter of 1838. The weapons soon proved their
efficacy, despite chain-firing tendencies and cap fragments
embedding themselves in the firers' faces.

The Paterson Revolvers were highly distinctive five-shot guns,
initially cocked by thumbing back the hammer to allow the trigger
to spring downwards from concealment in the frame. When firing
had been completed, the trigger was folded upwards to where it
could catch neither on clothing nor a holster. The calibres varied

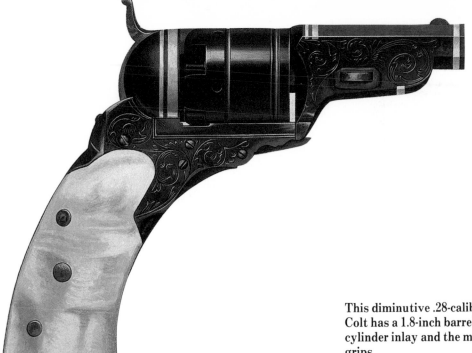

between .28 and .36, with barrel lengths between 1.8 and 12 inches; Pocket, Belt or Holster models were made, about 180 No.5 Holster Pistols being acquired by the government of the independent State of Texas in 1839-41. Though commonly associated with the 'Texas Navy', most were issued to the Texas Rangers.

Unfortunately, the Paterson Colt revolvers were clumsy and underpowered compared with the contemporaneous single-shot percussion pistols; they were too delicate to attract military attention and too expensive to sell commercially in great numbers. Most surviving guns date from 1839-40, virtually all displaying chamfered-edge chambers (Patent 1304 of August 1839) to minimize chain-firing. Some also display the rammers which allowed later Patersons to be reloaded without removing the cylinder.

The Patent Arms Manufacturing Company went into liquidation in 1842, and Colt's first venture had ended in disaster after six years. Many complete guns and thousands of parts were subsequently acquired by the former treasurer of the company, the unscrupulous John Ehlers, and new Paterson Colts were still being offered as late as 1847-8. In the spring of 1845, however, sale of the surviving machinery and tools ended the opening chapter of the Colt story.

Colt's early influence is continually contested by those who regard the inventor as a charlatan. Colt himself never claimed to have 'invented' the revolver: one surviving eight-shot snaphance revolver-carbine dates from 1597 and, had India-bound Colt stopped off in London in 1830-1, he may have encountered not only Collier guns – £10,000-worth of which had been sold in 1824-7 – but also old snaphance revolvers kept in the Tower of London. Guns made by John Dafte about 1680 and Thomas Annely (c.1710) often relied on cocking the hammer to revolve the cylinder.

That Colt managed to perfect a percussion revolver suited to mass production cannot be challenged. And the claim of Benjamin

Darling, who until his death maintained that he and his brother Barton had produced the first true mechanically-actuated American 'revolver', is weakened by the grant of his patent some two months *after* Colt's. Unfortunately, the U.S. Patent Office burned down in December 1836, incinerating the Colt and Darling models and all relevant papers.

Between 1836 and about 1844, the Darling Brothers marketed perhaps fewer than 250 pepperboxes provided by a number of small provincial gunmakers. These paltry quantities ensured the Darling design was eclipsed by a double-action bar-hammer pattern patented by Ethan Allen in 1837. The Allen was marketed in great style – to the detriment of Colt – into the 1840s, its popularity stemming from the speed with which it could be fired.

Another claimant to Colt's glory was Henry Humberger of Thorn Township, Ohio, who, with his brothers Adam and Peter, had produced a gun variously described as a 'revolver' or a 'pepperbox' in 1832. The *Thornville News* (October 1903) repeated a family claim that Colt had sent one of his 'shrewd and fine workmen' – John Pearson? – to purchase a Humberger gun from a dealer in 1834, inferring that Colt only succeeded in perfecting his revolver after seeing the Humbergers' design. Unfortunately, the confused newspaper article chronology greatly underplays the gap between the patenting of the Paterson Colt and the Massachusetts Arms Company litigation. Though its testimony is suspect and Colt's was the first patent, the trial depositions show that the Humberger brothers deserve much more attention than has previously been accorded.

Despite the failure of the Paterson venture, Colt remained convinced of the value of his invention. His chance of success came when Texas, the Lone Star State, was admitted into the Union in 1846. This change in political balance caused friction between the U.S.A. and Mexico, and an army under General Zachary Taylor was despatched to the Mexican border. Among the former Texas Rangers was Samuel H. Walker, who had had experience of the

The huge .44-calibre six-shot Walker Colt of 1847 weighed in excess of 4½lb.

This specially decorated Third Model Colt Dragoon revolver displays a Mexican snake-and-eagle crest on its ivory grip.

Seminole Wars under the command of Colonel Harney and was familiar with the Paterson Colts. Walker was commissioned captain in the U.S. Army and sent north to recruit more volunteers. He was also charged with obtaining more revolvers and immediately sought out Colt, to whom the patents had reverted. With Walker's co-operation, Colt refined the basic Paterson design, successfully tendering for a thousand-gun government contract in January 1847, and persuaded Eli Whitney – son of the cotton-gin inventor – to make the revolvers in his Whitneyville, Connecticut, factory.

Delivered in the Autumn of 1847, the enormous six-shot Walker Colts measured more than 15 inches overall and weighed in excess of 4.5 pounds. Though Walker fell to a Mexican lance-thrust at the battle of Juamantla in October 1847, his influence had been sufficient to re-establish Colt's fortunes.

The efficacy of the big Walker Colt soon brought an additional order, on the strength of which Colt established a new factory in Hartford in 1848. Here, from the Walker, Colt developed the first of the Model 1848 or Dragoon Revolvers. These initially embodied some old Whitney-made parts, but improvements were soon made and the second model featured pins between the nipples, a roller on the hammer and a leaf-type (rather than 'V'-type) mainspring. The Third Model Dragoon accepted a shoulder stock, supported by an extra screw through the frame, and its leaf-type back sight took advantage of the potentially steadier shooting position.

The Model 1848 and 1849 pocket revolvers, beloved by the miners lured by the great California gold rush of 1849, gave way to the classic .36-calibre Navy Colt. Generally known as the Model of 1851 or the Old Model Belt Pistol, this was smaller and neater than the Walkers or Dragoons, measuring a mere 13 inches overall and weighing only 2½ pounds. Nearly 250,000 Navies were made, excluding copies made in the Confederacy, Europe and elsewhere. Its 'navy' association came simply from the calibre and the naval scene rolled into the cylinder.

The Navy Colt assured the future. A massive new armoury was built in Hartford, on the banks of the Connecticut River, together with an ostentatious mansion named 'Armsmear'. Colt's Patent Fire Arms Manufacturing Company went from strength to strength; indeed, Colt's personal estate at his early death in 1862, hastened by overwork and rheumatic fever, has been estimated as 15 million dollars!

Much of the great success was due to Colt's longstanding friend

These ornate Colts, 1849 Pocket No. 63305 (*top*) and 1851 Navy No. 20131 (*above*) were presented to Russian Tsar Nikolai I in 1854.

Elisha Root. Root, who briefly succeeded to the presidency of the company before his own death in 1865, was a mechanical genius whose talents were normally employed in perfecting production machinery; however, he was also responsible for the maverick sidehammer revolvers and revolver-rifles introduced in 1855. Though these never attained the popularity of the larger Navy and Army patterns, they continued to appear in the company's catalogues until 1872. Their distinctive features included sheath triggers and hammers bent to clear the cylinder-retaining pin, which ran into the action from the rear. They were also the first of the Colts to feature a solid frame, chambered .28 and .31 calibre balls, had five-shot cylinders and round or octagonal barrels.

Colt's master patent, which expired in 1848, was renewed until 1855. It presented such a huge barrier that few rival guns were perfected until the mid 1850s. Typical of the failures was the Whitney Walking Beam revolver, optimistically patented by Fordyce Beals in September 1854, in which a ring trigger, a double ratchet and a beam system rotated the cylinder. Ironically, in an earlier ring-trigger patent, Whitney had drawn attention to the advantages of a solid frame – but neglected to add these to his claims and unwittingly allowed Remington to make a fortune. And in this period, all but unnoticed by Colt, came a bored-through cylinder patented by Rollin White in 1855.

Colt periodically took action against infringers of his patents. The most famous case was brought against the Massachusetts Arms

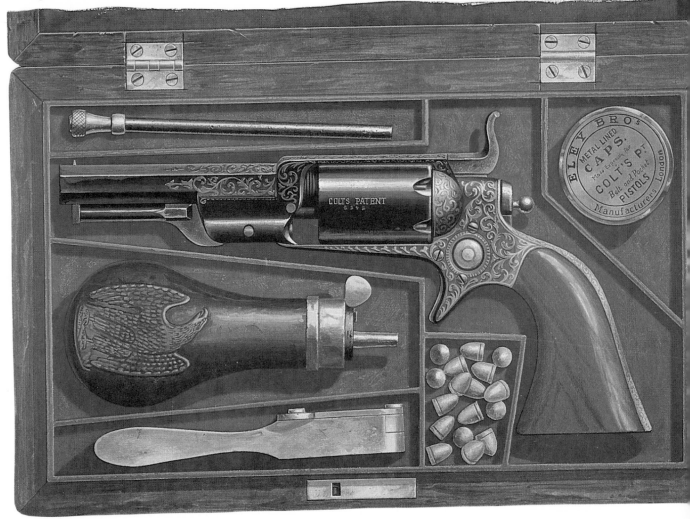

A cased Root Sidehammer Colt, No.10234, presented to Russian Grand-duke Mikhail Nikolaevich in 1858.

Company, which (as Wesson, Stevens & Miller) had made a few manually-operated revolvers under Daniel Leavitt's patent of April 1837. In 1847-8 the senior partner, Edwin Wesson, had designed a hammer that turned the cylinder through a bevel-gear. U.S. Patent 6669, granted in August 1849 after Wesson's death, was the basis on which the freshly incorporated Massachusetts Arms Company sought its fortune. Colt sued for patent infringement. After a show trial in which the foremost patent attorney of the day, Edwin Dickerson (for Colt), battled with one of the most colourful, Rufus Choate, the case went in Colt's favour largely because both guns used the hammer to turn the cylinder. As Colt's patent pre-dated Wesson's by thirteen years, the case cost the Massachusetts Arms Company $65,000 damages.

Colt's patents inhibited the establishment of a European revolver industry until the middle of the nineteenth century, though there were plenty of pepperboxes. Then things suddenly changed; not only did the British Colt patent expire in 1849, but the Patent Law Amendment Act of 1852 greatly reduced the fees necessary to protect an invention and precipitated a rush of applications. Though Colt established a factory in Bessborough Place, Millbank, near London's Vauxhall Bridge, he was never able to secure a monopoly.

At London's Great Exhibition in 1851, Colt had put on an impressive-looking display of machine-made arms; and when the doors finally closed, he astutely presented all the exhibits to influential people; one garniture (cased Dragoon and Navy Colts) was presented to Albert, the Prince Consort, and a 'Baby Dragoon' went to Edward, Prince of Wales (later Edward VII). At the exhibition, however, Colt's guns had received nothing more than a meritorious mention; prizes had been awarded to English gunmakers, however.

Destined to be a thorn in Colt's flesh for many years, the Adams revolver had been patented in Britain in February 1851 and had several superior features; its calibre was greater – 38, 54, 80 and 120 Bore – and the solid frame was stronger than Colt's ingenious wedge-retained open construction. The Adams also had a double-action trigger, rather than requiring thumb cocking for every shot. The Board of Ordnance subsequently acquired guns for trials and concluded that the Colt was preferable, having proved more accurate at long range and better made. But earlier tests undertaken for *The Times* had shown, according to Adams, that the converse was true where accuracy and rapidity of fire were concerned.

The advent of the Crimean War forced the British to purchase Navy Colts, taking approximately 23,560 between March 1854 and August 1855 in addition to private purchases. Despite Adams' protestations, only Colt could have provided so many guns in so short a time. Combat experience proved the Colonel's undoing; the .36-calibre bullet was such a poor manstopper that the balance of opinion swung back to the 38 Bore (.500) and 54 Bore (.442) Adams. By 1855, the latter had been improved by adding first Rigby's and then Kerr's patent rammers, and finally by incorporating lockwork patented by Lieutenant Frederick Beaumont of the Royal

Below: **The lockwork of the spurless-hammer Adams and the Beaumont-Adams revolvers.**

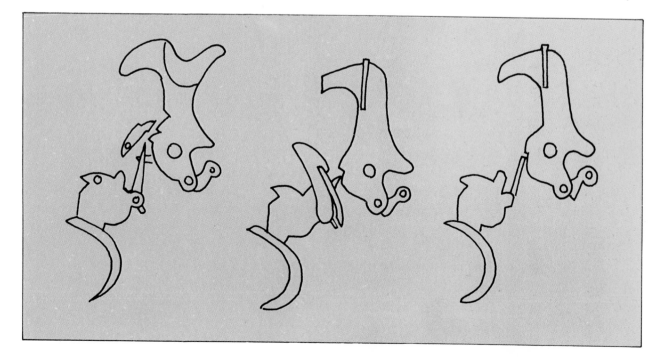

Engineers in February 1855. The addition of a rammer and a single-action hammer-spur, which had been the original Adams' weaknesses, persuaded the Board of Ordnance to substitute the Beaumont-Adams for the Colt. Some 19,123 were subsequently purchased officially between October 1855 and the end of 1860.

Unfortunately for Colt, the British gunmakers could not be accused of lacking innovative spirit. In the autumn of 1856, therefore, the closure of Colt's Millbank factory began and many of its skilled workmen returned to Hartford.

The British revolvers included the Single Action, 'Longspur', wedge and solid-frame Webleys. Officially termed the 'Improved Patent Repeating Pistol', the Longspur, patented in 1853, could be identified by its curiously elongated hammer. As its construction was generally weaker than Adams', it was soon superseded by wedge- and solid-frame guns based on a patent granted to Joseph Bentley in 1857. Introduced about 1861, the five- or six-shot Webley wedge-frames were made in 54, 90, 100 and 120 Bore. Another favourite with the Confederacy, the Kerr (54 and 80 Bore) was an

Above: **The Webley 'Longspur' revolver.**

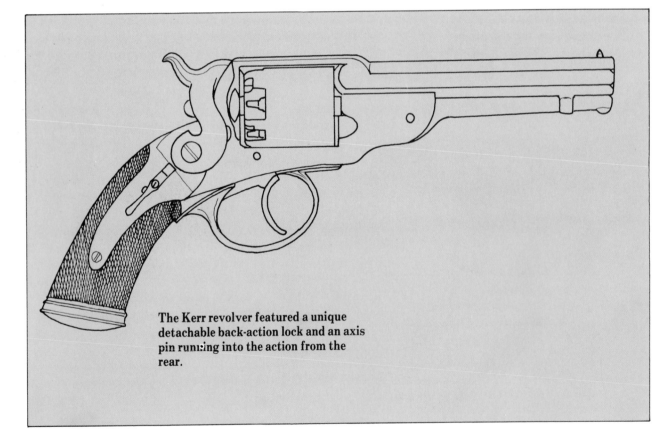

The Kerr revolver featured a unique detachable back-action lock and an axis pin running into the action from the rear.

odd sidehammer, patented in 1858-59, with a detachable back-action lockplate and a cylinder axis-pin entering from the rear. Nine hundred Kerr revolvers were landed at Wilmington, North Carolina, in October 1864; even the Federal government purchased sixteen from Schuyler, Hartley & Graham in the dark days of 1861.

Patented in 1853, the original Tranter superficially resembled the Adams – but had a hinged rammer on the left side of the frame and a unique double-trigger system in which a pull on the spur protruding beneath the trigger guard cocked the hammer. The hammer was then released by squeezing the trigger lever protruding ahead of the spur-body. Birmingham-made Tranters came in several different calibres from 38 to 120 Bore, and enjoyed some years in vogue until a single-trigger variant was patented in 1859. Other guns included Webley-Bentley self-cockers, often found with an 1854-patent screw rammer; and the open-frame Daw, based on Lang and then Pryse & Cashmore patents.

The problem was simply that no British gunmaker could mass-produce guns, relying instead on traditional but notoriously ineffectual sub-contracting methods. Adams revolvers, for example, involved not only Adams and his successor (Deane, Adams & Deane) but also William Tranter, Hollis & Sheath and Joseph Brazier of Birmingham. In Europe, though the licence was apparently negotiated solely with Francotte of Liége, three other Belgian subcontractors seem to have been recruited. Even when the London Armoury Company began to make the Beaumont-Adams in 1856, production initially proceeded on traditional lines.

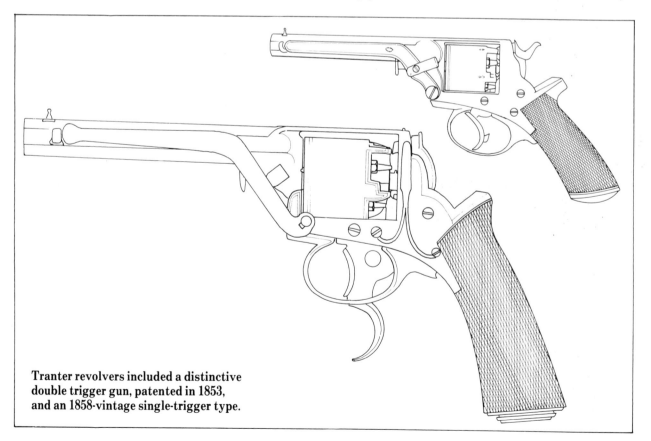

Tranter revolvers included a distinctive double trigger gun, patented in 1853, and an 1858-vintage single-trigger type.

The Adams and its British rivals prevented the establishment of a Colt monopoly in Britain. Anxious to promote his design in Europe, Colt licensed production of the Dragoon model in Europe, where modified copies were made in Austria and Belgium. After the agreements had lapsed, many thousands of unlicensed piracies were also made in Belgium. However, there was always a small-calibre pinfire to challenge the European percussion revolver. No matter how fragile and dangerous it could be, the metallic-case pinfire cartridge undoubtedly had something to offer; as it was relatively waterproof, the gun could be left laden without the worry of non-ignition caused by damp. And the smallest pinfire revolvers were ridiculously cheap.

The American Civil War of 1861-65 was a dreadful struggle between South and North, though the slavery question was often subordinated to fierce regional patriotism. But enthusiasm for war was soon replaced by a determination not to be beaten, and the bitter struggle lasted four years. The handguns used in the Civil War were not confined to Colt, even though the elegant .44-calibre Model 1860, or New Model Army Pistol, had appeared shortly before the war began. The Federal government purchased the products of fourteen manufacturers, while the output of countless

Above: Engraved by Gustave Young, .44-calibre 1860 Army Colt No.31906 was one of a pair presented to the King of Sweden in 1863.

Below: A Starr .44 single-action revolver, made towards the end of the American Civil War.

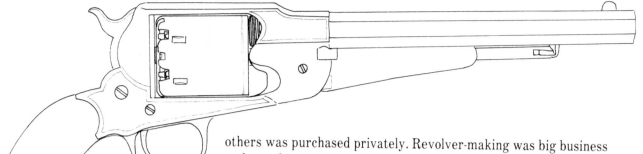

others was purchased privately. Revolver-making was big business and a crafty entrepreneur could make huge sums of money; indeed, the government's purchases fell only a little short of six million dollars' worth – a huge sum in the mid nineteenth century – and at least five million more were spent by state militia, wealthy sponsors of 'private' regiments and relatives of individual conscripts.

Colts accounted for 39 per cent of the total government acquisition in 1861-6, which was only fractionally greater than purchases of Remingtons (35 per cent); the next most numerous class, the rather odd-looking Starrs, accounted for only some 13 per cent. Most of the Colts were the 1860 or army model, 129,730 of which were acquired, though there were 17,010 .36-calibre Navy

Above and below: The .44-calibre Remington New Army percussion revolver.

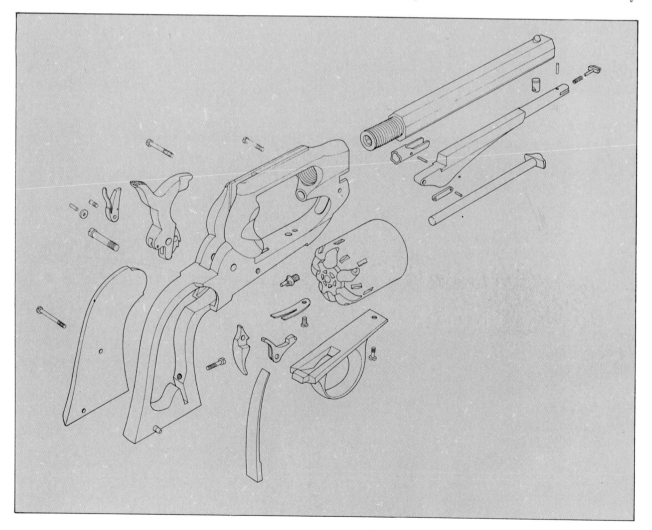

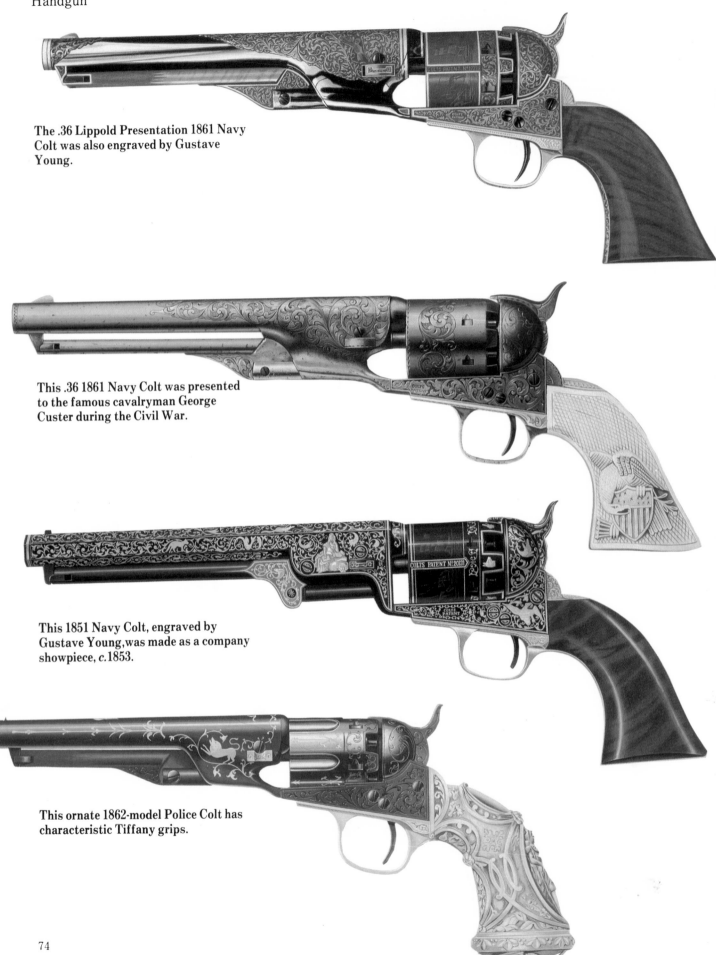

The .36 Lippold Presentation 1861 Navy Colt was also engraved by Gustave Young.

This .36 1861 Navy Colt was presented to the famous cavalryman George Custer during the Civil War.

This 1851 Navy Colt, engraved by Gustave Young, was made as a company showpiece, c.1853.

This ornate 1862-model Police Colt has characteristic Tiffany grips.

The Savage revolver, with its unique heart-shape guard, was one of the most distinctive Civil War revolvers.

Models. A particularly beautiful 1860-pattern .44 Army revolver was presented to King Carl XV Gustav of Sweden in an attempt to prevent Swedish spars and masts gracing Confederate blockade runners; and another went to King Frederik of Denmark in an attempt to stop Danish weapons reaching the Confederacy.

Remington provided 125,314 .44-calibre Remington New Model Army Revolvers, based on Beals' and Rider's patents, which offered the advantages of solid-frame construction. These guns were strong and effectual, though manufacturing quality was generally reckoned below Colt's. However, despite being comparable in size and power with the 1860 Army Colt, the Remington cost only $13.02 against $17.70 for its rival.

The Starrs were based on patents granted to Ebenezer Starr in 1858. This double-action revolver came through its early U.S. Army tests with flying colours, eliciting some impressive testimonials. The government bought small quantities of the .36-calibre version and then a larger number of the .44 pattern; however, as the Civil War ran its course, a single-action .44 appeared to accelerate production. Total procurement in the period between New Year's Day 1861 and 30 June 1866 amounted to 47,952.

The remainder of the official purchases were restricted to comparatively small numbers. The most numerous indigenous guns were the Savage and Whitney designs, a little over 11,000 of each being acquired. Freeman-patent army revolvers were made by C.B. Hoard's Armory of Watertown, New York, but only about 2,500 were delivered to Freeman's agents before the contract for 5,000 was cancelled in favour of Rogers & Spencer revolvers. There were also 2,814 Beals revolvers; 2,001 of the curious striker fired Pettengills, based on patents granted to Pettengill, Robitaille and

The Confederacy's Le Mat revolver had a .67-calibre shot barrel doubling as a cylinder axis-pin.

Confederate dead lie on Marye's Heights, Fredericksburg, after the Battle of Chancellorsville in 1863.

Raymond in 1856-59 (but made by Rogers & Spencer); 1,100 Joslyn revolvers, invented by Benjamin Joslyn of Stonington, Connecticut; and 536 Allens. Among the imports were nearly 13,000 Lefaucheux pinfires, plus a few British Beaumont-Adams, French Raphaels, and Perrins with their distinctive thick-rimmed rimfire cartridges.

Not all of these guns were successful. The sidehammer Joslyn, for example, had a particularly odd history. Its first manufacturer – W.C. Freeman of Worcester, Massachusetts – refused to deliver an 'unserviceable design' to the U.S. Army and instead sold completed guns to the wholesale trade, which passed them to the Ohio state militia in 1861; after Joslyn had established his own factory in Stonington, Connecticut, some 875 .44-calibre revolvers were delivered to the Federal government in 1862 and 675 more went to Ohio. Interestingly, the Ohio militia rejected the Joslyns, which ended their days in Federal stores.

As a final twist, many Joslyns were recovered from the 'Sons of Liberty' after an unsuccessful attempt to free Confederate prisoners from Camp Douglas, near Springfield, and then seize Illinois and Indiana. Though guns probably came via Canada, Joslyn may have been selling to both sides concurrently! Two thousand Butterfield-patent disc-primed revolvers made by Krider in Philadelphia had already found their way to the Confederacy after

A Union trench on Kennesaw Mountain, Georgia, during the American Civil War. This was a new environment in which percussion revolvers had to work efficiently; damp and mud ensured they did not.

being ordered by the 5th New York Cavalry.

The Confederacy had a much poorer arms industry than the Federals, most resources being concentrated north of the Mason-Dixon Line. However, modified Dragoon or Navy Colts were made by the Augusta Machine Works; the Columbus Fire Arms Co.; Dance Bros. & Parks; L. Tucker & Co., its successor Tucker, Sherrard & Co.; and then Clark Sherrard & Company. None of these made more than a few hundred. However, Griswold & Gunnison of Griswoldville, Georgia, made 3,000; and Leech & Rigdon, Leech & Co., and Rigdon, Ansley & Co. made about 1,500 in Columbus, Greensboro and Augusta. Spiller & Burr of Atlanta and then Macon, Georgia, made about 1,500 Whitney copies in 1862-4. At the other extreme, about twenty brass-framed Remington-Beals type revolvers were made by farmer Alfred Kapp of Sisterdale, Texas.

The pitifully meagre indigenous production forced the Confederacy to depend on captured weapons, or British and French revolvers. The most interesting of these guns was undoubtedly the Le Mat; patented by Alexandre le Mat of New Orleans in October 1856, the standard wartime revolvers – made in France and Britain – substitute a .67-calibre shot barrel for the cylinder axis pin and have a selector mounted on the hammer-nose. A metallic-cartridge version was patented in 1869 by Le Mat's son, François Alexandre.

5. The Colonel's Legacy

If you value your safety, never use a revolver whose hammer rests on or opposite the firing pin, or whose hammer, in firing, does not strike the firing pin direct. The former is dangerous. The latter is uncertain.

Among the merits of the Hopkins & Allen Arms Company's 'Triple Action Safety Police Revolver', from a 1907-vintage company broadsheet.

Handgun design was in a state of flux in the years after the American Civil War. Percussion revolvers had been very successful, though no great future lay ahead of them: unreliable, messy and prone to chain-firing unless carefully loaded, they were doomed by the perfection of the metallic cartridge.

The most important of the early revolvers was the Smith & Wesson Model 1, based on a patent granted to Rollin White in April 1855; thanks to an extension, this remained enforceable until 1872 and effectively halted the progress of all rival designs. An agreement reached in November 1856 left poor White responsible for bringing each patent infringement case, eating so greatly into his royalties that he predictably lost interest in firearms and invented the White Steam Car.

The original White percussion-ignition revolver had an automatic primer feed. Each time the rammer was operated, a linen cartridge fed into the cylinder from a magazine above the breech. However, the most important feature of this otherwise unremarkable design was a bored-through cylinder, the protection of which prevented rival manufacturers marketing effectual breech-loaded revolvers. Ironically, Eugène Lefaucheux had patented a similar pin-fire revolver cylinder in France in 1854, but his patent was invalid in the U.S.A.

The pocket-size .22 rimfire S&W Model 1, introduced late in 1858, had a lifting barrel hinged at the top front of the frame. Its cylinder could be removed, and the spent cases punched out on a fixed ejector rod under the barrel. About 11,000 Model 1 'First Issue' revolvers were made in 1858-9, and an enlarged factory was completed in the spring of 1860 to make a modified version. The American Civil War was a great boost to Smith & Wesson's operations, as the .22 rimfire Model 1 and .32 rimfire Model 2 were popular personal defence guns. Production of the Models 1, 1½ and 2 totalled 320,000 between 1858 and 1882.

Until the Rollin White patent finally expired in 1872, other

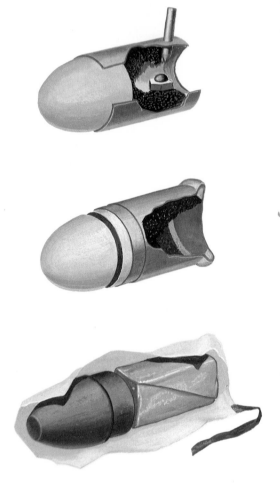

The three principal cartridges current in 1860. Top, a pinfire; middle, a rimfire; and bottom, the standard combustible paper-case pattern.

The cylinder and breech of the Colt revolver, with the hammer at full-cock. Note the brasswork.

American inventors had to struggle with an extraordinary collection of evasions. These included a .42-calibre six-shot cup primer gun, often called 'Merwin & Bray' after one of its principal distributors but made by Plant's Manufacturing Company of New Haven (1863-5) and the Eagle Arms Company (1865-7) to the patents of Willard Ellis and John White (1859-63). Another front-loading teat-fire cartridge, patented by David Williamson in January 1864, was fired in the .32-calibre six-shot sheath trigger revolver initially made by the Moore Patent Fire Arms Company and then by National Arms Company until the latter was absorbed by Colt in 1870.

In October 1865 Silas Crispin patented a unique vertically split cylinder, the front part of which moved forward when the barrel was unlatched. This was subsequently incorporated in a rarely seen .32 revolver made by the Smith Arms Company of New York. Patented in April 1863, the .32 rimfire five-shot Slocum (often known as the 'Brooklyn' after its manufacturer) had sliding sleeves on each chamber; standard rimfire cartridges could be dropped in from the side, circumventing Rollin White's patent. Another evasion was the 1863 patent of John Vickers and Lucius Pond, in which a rimfire

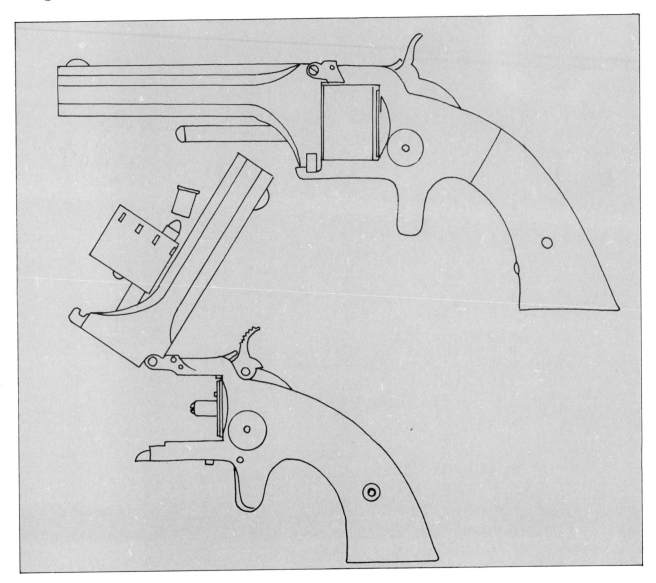

The .22 rimfire Smith & Wesson Model 1 had an unusual barrel-pivot system.

cartridge, inserted in a special sleeve, was then inserted in the front of the specially bored-out cylinder.

Colt's influence in Europe was less spectacular. Revolvers were still regarded with suspicion in the mid-nineteenth century – a legacy, no doubt, of the ineffectual pepperboxes and fragile open-frame 'transition' guns. And while the Continent took to Colt's pocket revolvers quite readily, and many thousands were made in Liége and Paris, a pinfire competitor offering a self-contained (if fragile and dangerous) metallic cartridge was always to be had for a few francs. As European military authorities were rarely as convinced of the merits of the revolver as the Civil War Americans had been, introduction of such guns was often considerably delayed. Even then they were often regarded more as a badge of rank than weapons.

The principal European metallic cartridge revolver was the Lefaucheux pinfire, which remained popular for fifty years. The first gun was patented in France by Eugène Lefaucheux in 1854 and adopted by the French navy in 1858; similar, if generally smaller,

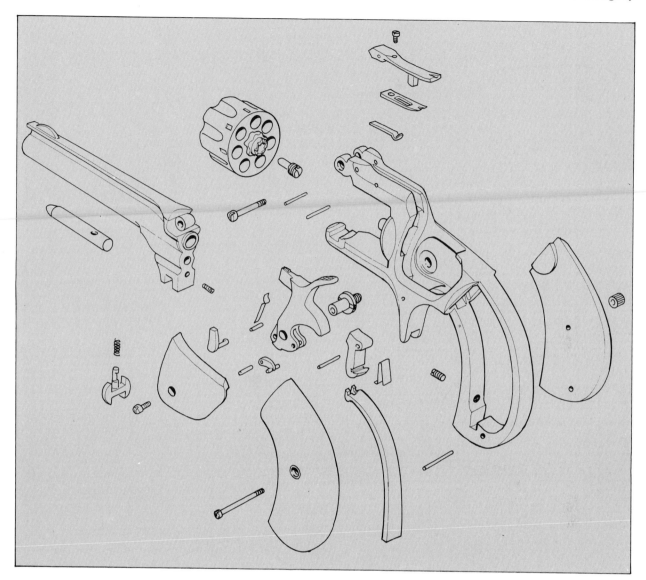

guns were made by a variety of manufacturers until the beginning of World War I. The navy Lefaucheux was an impressive-looking large calibre gun, but though its self-contained brass case impressed the French, there was still relatively little power. In addition, the weakness of the exposed-pin ignition system – cartridges were vulnerable even to an oblique blow – curtailed its military career prematurely. By 1870, several acceptable centrefire designs had gained military acceptance.

The first large-calibre Smith & Wesson, a sheath trigger solid-frame prototype, was rejected by the U.S. Army in 1865. However, after successfully converting several thousand Remington percussion revolvers to rimfire in 1868, the company developed an auto-extracting top-break revolver. As this infringed existing patents, Smith & Wesson sensibly bought the two 1865-vintage simultaneous extractor designs of W.C. Dodge; Louis Rodier's cylinder-rotating ratchet (also patented in 1865); and the cylinder, barrel and recoil shield combination designed by Abram Gibson in 1860. Patents for the new S&W Model 3 were granted in 1869.

An exploded view of the modernized Smith & Wesson top-break revolver, with a bird's head butt.

The prototype .44-calibre top-break Smith & Wesson Model 3 was submitted to the U.S. Army in 1870. Apart from recommending a change from rim- to centrefire, the Board of Ordnance and Fortification reportedly considered the revolver 'superior to any other . . . submitted'. The cartridge was duly changed, becoming the S&W .44/100, and production began – a great milestone in the development of the handgun. The Smith & Wesson was among the first to feature an effectual top-break hinged frame and a powerful extractor through the central axis of the cylinder to kick out even the most recalcitrant fired case.

Sample guns were immediately sent to the U.S. Army and the Russian military attaché, General Aleksandr Gorlov, who was supervising the acceptance of Colt-made Berdan rifles. At the end of December 1870, the U.S. Army ordered 1,000 Model 3 army revolvers; the Russians ordered 20,000 modified guns in May 1871. The Russian ordnance had insisted on a major change in the bullet diameter, reducing it below the diameter of the case and necessitating a stepped rather than parallel-bored chamber. However, accuracy was greatly improved and muzzle velocity rose by 100 feet per second.

Apart from chambering and cyrillic barrel-top inscriptions, the .44/100 'American' and .44 S&W Russian variants of the Model 3 were identical. It has been claimed that development of the latter and its cartridge resulted from the presentation of an ornate pearl-handled Model 3 to the Russian Grand Duke Alexei, but Alexei's visit actually occurred seven months *after* the cartridge had been redesigned and the contract had been signed.

In January 1873, the Russians signed a contract for 20,000 modified second or infantry-pattern S&W Model 3 revolvers (subsequently called 'Old old model' by the factory), with hump-back frames and a finger spur beneath the trigger guard. This and a third or cavalry pattern were made concurrently until the final contracts of May 1877. And though it is claimed that Smith & Wesson accepted 'a large contract for 215,000 guns', purchases of the three differing models totalled only 131,138; none of the individual contracts exceeded 20,000. Including commercial guns, sales to Turkey and Japan, and the Schofield variant, total production of these .44 S&W top-breaks in 1870-1912 amounted to about 250,000.

While Smith & Wesson prospered, the Rollin White patent hamstrung Colt into reliance on the ineffectual Thuer tapered-

Below: Smith & Wesson's Model 3, .44 American revolver with its shoulder stock.

Above: **The Moore teat-fire revolver cartridge contained priming in the protruding nipple at the rear of the case.**

cartridge system, patented in 1868, and then the 1871 Mason metallic-cartridge conversion. However, once S&W had accepted the Russian contract, the way was left open for Colt to dominate the domestic market.

The so-called 'Model 1872' Colt was an open top version of the 1860-pattern percussion-ignition army revolver firing rimfire cartridges. After this interim design came the 'Model P', or Peacemaker. Though this gun had several flaws compared with Smith & Wesson's effectual Russian model, the Colt was simpler, stronger and virtually impossible to wreck. Though the fixed firing pin forced guns to be holstered with the hammer down on an empty chamber, for fear of accidental ignition, the Model P was such a success that it remained in production until 1940. By then, production had amounted to 310,386 standard guns, 44,350 of the highly distinctive Bisley models with lowered hammers and differing frames, and a handful of flat-top target revolvers. There had also been thirty chamberings ranging in popularity from 158,885 .45 Long Colt guns down to a unique .32 rimfire specimen. The 71,391 revolvers chambering .44-40 were particularly popular among Westerners, permitting a Colt revolver and a Winchester rifle to share the same ammunition.

The Colt's reputation was helped incalculably by its adoption for the U.S. Army in 1873. Though the Peacemaker had beaten its rivals in the trials of 1873, including several Smith & Wessons, the appearance of a gun incorporating modifications suggested by Major George Schofield of the 10th Cavalry (patented in June 1871 and April 1873) proved more of a problem. By simplifying the extracting system and moving the locking latch from the barrel extension to the standing frame, Schofield had altered the S&W Model 3 specifically for cavalrymen.

After a trial in which the S&W was declared equal or superior to all its rivals, including the Colt Model 1873, the Army ordered 3,000 Schofields as the 'Model of 1875'. The total acquisition by 1879 being

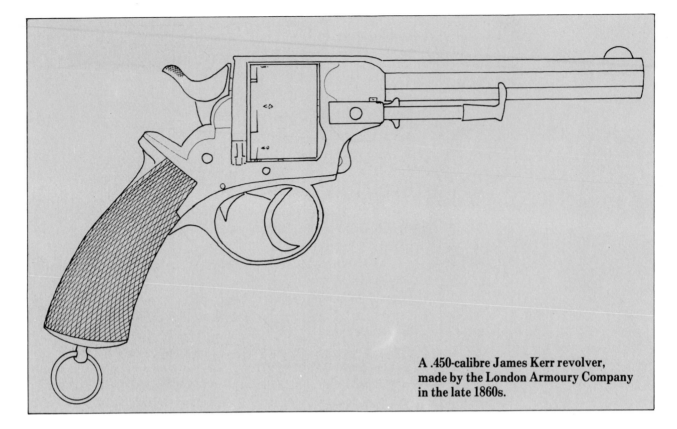

A .450-calibre James Kerr revolver,
made by the London Armoury Company
in the late 1860s.

Above: A massive Belgian 20-shot
pinfire revolver. The promoters of these
guns emphasized firepower rather than
clumsiness!

8,285, compared with 20,073 Model 1873 Colts. The disaster at the
Little Big Horn led to claims that, as the S&W Schofield was easier
to load than the Colt, the outcome of the battle could have been
different. One test showed that an experienced cavalryman
galloping on horseback could reload the S&W in less than thirty
seconds, while the Colt took a minute of undivided concentration.

Unfortunately, S&W had chambered the Schofield Model for a
special short cartridge, reducing velocity compared with the .45
Long Colt and compromising accuracy. And while the Colt revolver
would fire both rounds, the S&W could not fire the standard Colt
cartridge: problems arose as soon as Colt cartridges were delivered
to Schofield-armed troops. Together with the undoubted simplicity
of the Colt, this forced the army to standardise the Model P and the
Schofield was abandoned. Its inventor unhappily took his life with
one of his own guns in the winter of 1882. Ironically, within fifteen
years, cavalrymen were clamouring for a gun that could be loaded
faster than the Model 1873.

The success of the Peacemaker, the unavailability of the .44 Smith
& Wesson commercially and, perhaps most importantly, the
exposure given the Colt in western fiction and cowboy films now
tends to mask the others' successes. Between 1875 and 1900, Smith
& Wesson also made the sheath-trigger 'Baby Russian', or .38 Single

Colonel George A. Custer, pictured in Montana in the early 1870s with some of his Colt-carrying scouts.

Action (1876-77); the externally similar .38 SA Second Model (1877-91) and the .38 SA Third Model (1890-1911) with a conventional trigger guard. About 161,000 of these guns were made alongside nearly 100,000 of the smaller .32 Single Action (1877-92). More interesting were the various .32, .38 and .44 Double Action models. At least thirteen patterns of these were made between 1880 and 1920, selling nearly a milion between them. Similar .32 and .38 'Safety Hammerless' or New Departure models, with shrouded hammers and grip safeties, were first made in July 1886. A little over 500,000 had been made by 1940.

The Smith & Wesson double-action .32 and .38 revolvers gave the company an important technical lead over Colt at a time when the latter could only offer limited numbers of No.1 and No.2 deringers, acquired by purchasing the National Arms Company of Brooklyn, and the Thuer-designed No.3, 45,000 of which sold between 1875 and 1912. Early in the 1870s, these had been joined by the Cloverleaf House pistol – the first Colt to be made specifically for metallic cartridges – and the popular Open Top Pocket Pistol. The New Line guns developed by William Mason in 1873-4 came in five calibres, five frame-sizes and five serial ranges, about 108,000 selling between 1874 and 1886. By 1893, and the introduction of the .32 New Pocket revolver with a swing-out cylinder, Colt regained the lead from Smith & Wesson. Though only 30,000 New Pockets sold between 1893 and 1905, they paved the way for a series of similar guns that included the .32 Pocket Positive, 130,000 of which were made in 1905-43, the .32 Police Positive (199,000, 1905-43) and the .38 Police Positive Special (750,000, 1908-74 and 1977-80).

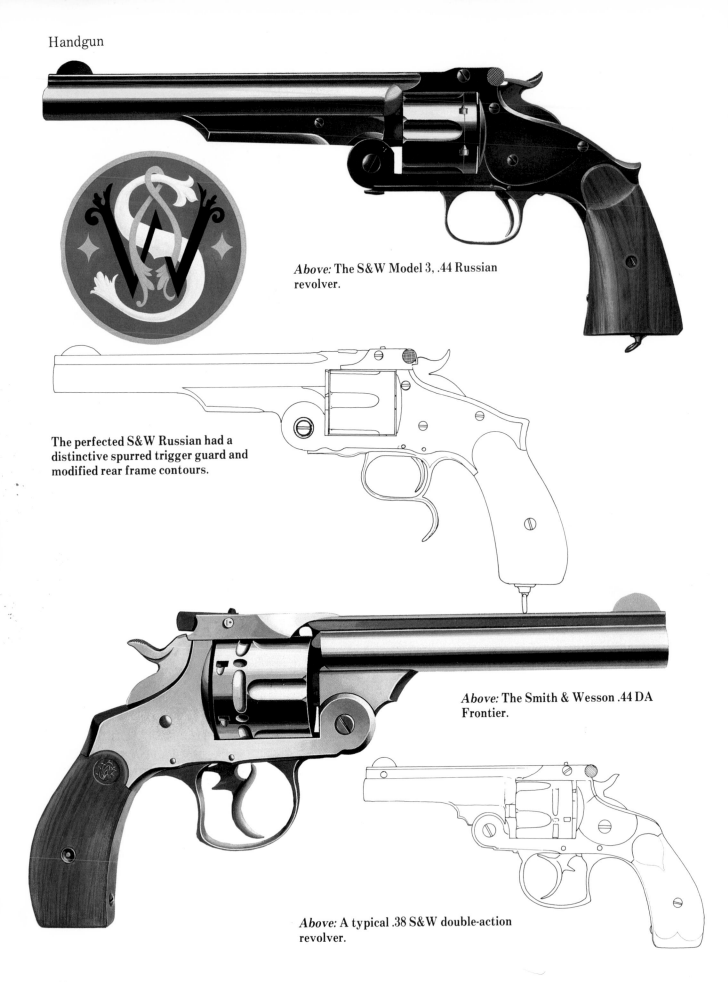

Above: The S&W Model 3, .44 Russian revolver.

The perfected S&W Russian had a distinctive spurred trigger guard and modified rear frame contours.

Above: The Smith & Wesson .44 DA Frontier.

Above: A typical .38 S&W double-action revolver.

The standard cavalry issue Colt Peacemaker had a 7½-inch barrel and plain wooden grips.

A .44 S&W Russian Colt Peacemaker, No.242701.

Made in 1897, this Colt Peacemaker, No.172485, features a Sears, Roebuck & Co. 'Liberty' grip.

Colt's Peacemaker was continuing to sell well, though, in relation to the output of Smith & Wesson, it is interesting to note that only 182,000 Peacemakers had been made by the end of 1899. The U.S. Army had taken a little over 37,000 (1873-91), though only 30,000 had actually been issued. In 1877, Colt announced the .38 Lightning, with new double-action lockwork and a bird's head butt. The gun's delicate lockwork has often been justifiably criticized, but outlaws such as William Bonney ('Billy the Kid') showed that the Lightning was not without utility; indeed, 167,000 .38 Lightnings and .41 Thunderers had been made by 1909, together with 51,000 heavier .45 Double Action Frontiers (or Model of 1878). In 1902, the U.S. Army acquired 4,600 of the so-called Alaskan model of the DA Frontier with a deep trigger guard to allow either two fingers or a thickly gloved finger to enter.

A contemporary Smith & Wesson advertisement, emphasizing the merits of the single-action revolvers.

A .41 Colt New Army revolver, made about 1903.

Above: **A decorative variant of the Colt Deringer No.3.**

This .44-40 Colt Peacemaker, No.100381, was shipped westward in October 1883.

In the early 1880s, Colt began to experiment with solid-frame guns and side-swinging cylinders. Most of the work is credited to the prolific William Mason and, after Mason had departed for Winchester, to Carl Ehbets. The first tangible result was the U.S. Navy Revolver Model of 1889, which inspired a series of similar military models (1892-1903). Their quirky anti-clockwise cylinder rotation has been blamed on the original naval testing commission; unfortunately, as the cylinder also swings out to the left, wear in the action inevitably causes misalignment between the chamber and the bore. However, 322,000 were made before the Army Special & Official Police Model of 1908 reverted to clockwise rotation.

Where Colt led, Smith & Wesson had to follow; the first S&W Hand Ejector was actually built on a Model 1892 Colt army revolver frame. Perfected revolvers were placed on the market in 1896, but sales were initially slow; less than 20,000 examples of the .32 Hand Ejector Model of 1896 were made with the small 'I' frame, though the improved 1903 pattern, which remained in production until 1942, sold more than half a million. The .32/20 and .38 Hand Ejector revolvers, introduced in 1899 on the 'K' frame, lasted into the 1940s; production of the latter reached a million.

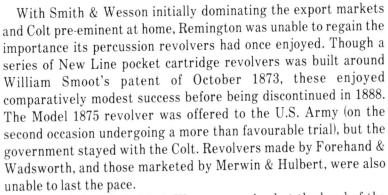

With Smith & Wesson initially dominating the export markets and Colt pre-eminent at home, Remington was unable to regain the importance its percussion revolvers had once enjoyed. Though a series of New Line pocket cartridge revolvers was built around William Smoot's patent of October 1873, these enjoyed comparatively modest success before being discontinued in 1888. The Model 1875 revolver was offered to the U.S. Army (on the second occasion undergoing a more than favourable trial), but the government stayed with the Colt. Revolvers made by Forehand & Wadsworth, and those marketed by Merwin & Hulbert, were also unable to last the pace.

Though Colt and Smith & Wesson remained at the head of the market in 1900, the work of lesser companies should not be undervalued. Of these, Harrington & Richardson of Worcester, Massachusetts, formed in 1871 as 'Wesson & Harrington', was remarkable for its Shell Ejector revolver of 1871 – the first American cartridge pattern with an auto-ejecting system. The first H&R double-action gun appeared in 1878, the precursor of similar guns lasting well into the twentieth century. Iver Johnson revolvers

Above: **The Remington M1875 revolver, externally resembling the Colt Peacemaker.**

William Sprague's curved-barrel butt-cylinder revolver. American, 1888.

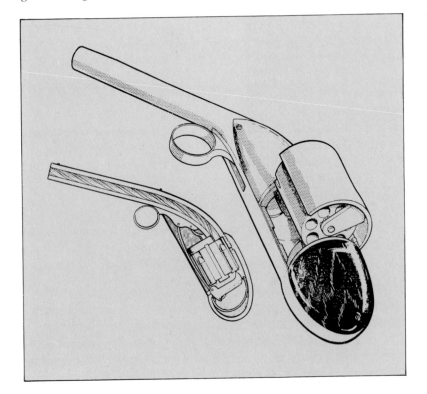

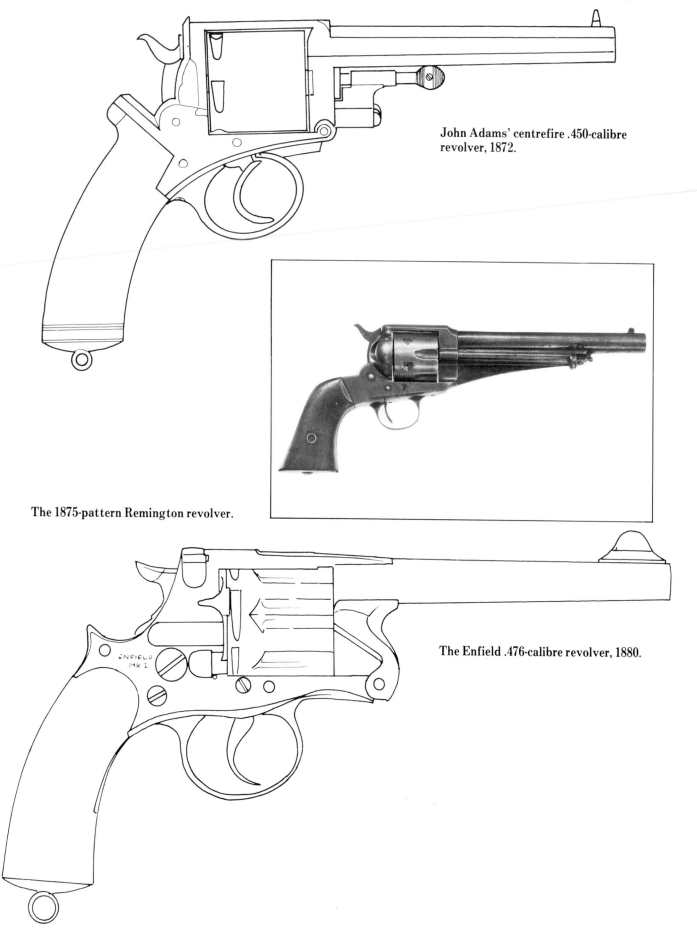

John Adams' centrefire .450-calibre revolver, 1872.

The 1875-pattern Remington revolver.

The Enfield .476-calibre revolver, 1880.

were marketed exclusively by the Lovell Arms Company of Boston, Massachusetts, from 1871 until 1895. The first double-action pocket revolver, known as the Eagle, appeared in 1878 and was eventually followed by the famous 'Hammer-the-Hammer' system, designed by Andrew Fyrberg about 1896, patented in 1900 but not advertised with any force until 1904. A 'lifter' or transfer bar, which can only be raised by deliberate pressure on the trigger, enabled the hammer to be struck as hard as possible with no chance of the chambered cartridge firing. The recessed hammer face strikes the inertia type firing pin only when the lifter is interposed. The 'Hammer-the-Hammer' mechanism provided such a strong source of advertising potential that Iver Johnson had become the world's largest producer of revolvers by 1910.

The last quarter of the nineteenth century was the heyday of the 'Suicide (or Saturday) Specials' – cheap single-action sheath trigger revolvers, the best of which were made by companies such as Marlin and Hopkins & Allen, but the worst of which went unsigned by virtue of their uniformly poor construction. They were usually grandly named – from the 'Aetna', made by Harrington & Richardson, to Hopkins & Allen's 'XL'.

Even in the last quarter of the nineteenth century, the British gunsmiths, though occasionally banding together to handle government contracts, were happiest when working individually. This hindered progress well into the present century – though, paradoxically, failed to prevent P. Webley & Sons and its successor,

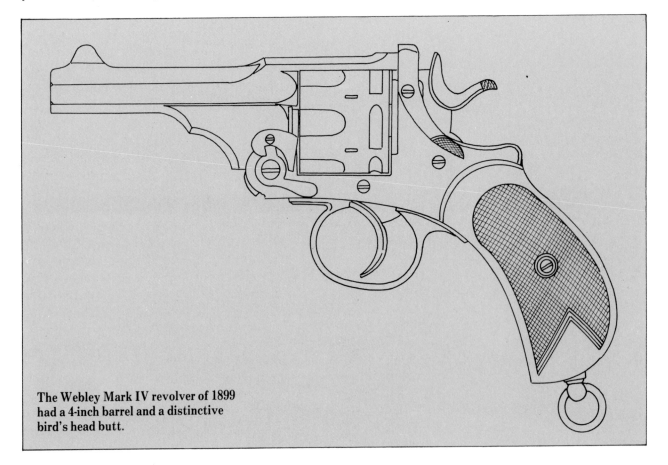

The Webley Mark IV revolver of 1899 had a 4-inch barrel and a distinctive bird's head butt.

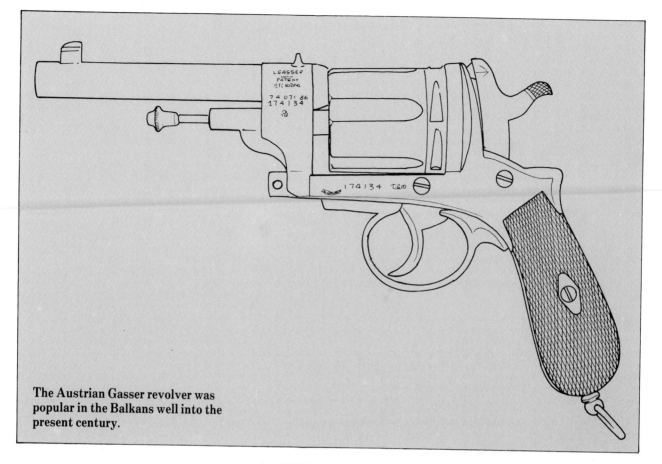

The Austrian Gasser revolver was popular in the Balkans well into the present century.

the Webley & Scott Revolver & Arms Company, monopolizing the production of cartridge revolvers. In 1879, when 500 assorted Tranter, Webley and Colt revolvers were acquired to supplement the existing Adams conversions, nearly a quarter of the delivery was rejected by government viewers. However, the Royal Small Arms Factory at Enfield had already begun to design a .476-calibre revolver that could be made in the government factory. The result combined an auto-extracting system credited to a Welsh-born Philadelphian named Owen Jones with lockwork adapted from Warnant and Kaufmann patents.

Adopted in August 1880, the 'Pistol, Breech Loading, Enfield, Mark 1' was loaded through a hinged gate on the right side of the breech and extracted fired cases (but not unfired rounds) by pivoting the barrel downwards on its bracket. This pulled the cylinder longitudinally forwards on the cylinder arbor, leaving the cases held on a fixed star-plate in the breech. Empty cases then simply fell out of the gun. The Enfield had other interesting features: the chamber-mouths were rifled and the lockwork was nickel-plated. Unfortunately, service soon showed a number of severe defects. Flaked-off plating often jammed the mechanism, the lowermost case often failed to clear the breech without the cylinder being revolved manually, and the rifled chamber mouths – which rarely aligned with the bore properly – often choked with lead fragments. An improved Mark II was adopted in 1881 and a safety catch, rather belatedly approved in the summer of 1887, was not added to production guns until 1889. By this time, the clumsy and inaccurate Enfield was already out of favour.

Webley had made large numbers of the strong but otherwise unremarkable solid-frame 'RIC' (Royal Irish Constabulary) revolver from 1867 onwards, chambering cartridges as large as .476, but was experimenting with break-open guns by the late 1870s. The Webley-Pryse revolver of 1877 amalgamated a rebounding hammer and twin spring-loaded breech-locking arms, credited to Charles Pryse the Younger, with a hinged frame patented by Edward Wood.

The Pryse revolver, made by Webley and (among others) Francotte of Liége, was soon refined by way of the Webley-Kaufmann and the Webley-Green – or 'Webley Government' – into the .442 six-shot revolver adopted by the British Army in 1887. The principal improvement was the addition of a stirrup-type breech catch on the left side of the frame, where it could be actuated simply by pushing forward with the thumb of the firing hand. John Carter, a 'gun action filer' of Aston juxta Birmingham, had patented this design in 1885; shortly after the Webley had been accepted for government service, a Cheltenham gunmaker named Edwinson Green claimed to have originated the system in 1883. An unconvincing 'rebuttal' by Webley subsequently appeared in *The Field* in 1889, but Green apparently then took Webley to court, implying that Carter had known about the plaintiff's design prior to the application for Patent 4070 of 1885. Webley then settled with Green out of court; as the new revolver was such an attractive proposition, the company wisely did not wish to jeopardise a contract for 10,000 signed in July 1887. The pattern arm was sealed in November and the first issues were eventually made in 1892.

The Continental European giant of the early 1870s was Chamelot, Delvigne et Cie of Liége, whose robust and reliable revolvers

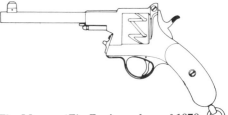

The Mauser 'Zig-Zag' revolver of 1878 used cam-tracks to revolve its cylinder.

Left: **The Japanese 26th Year Type revolver (1893) showed distinct Smith & Wesson influence.**

Nagant's gas-seal revolver was especially popular in Russia, where it was adopted in 1895.

Above: **Mauser's solid-frame 1878-vintage revolver.**

became the classic European design. Adopted in France, Belgium, The Netherlands, Switzerland, Italy and Portugal, some guns were rimfire and others centrefire; survivors were still being encountered on active service during World War II. However, by the 1880s, the supremacy of the Chamelot-Delvigne system was challenged by that of the Nagant Brothers, Léon and Emile, of Liége. If the Chamelot-Delvigne revolvers were the pattern of the 1870s, then the Nagants were the archetype of the 1880s. Copied (like their predecessors) by countless gunsmiths, usually without benefit of licence, the design was very successful. The Belgian army purchased the Models 1878, 1878/86 (officer's) and 1883; Luxembourg took the Model 1884, the constabulary version of which had a bayonet; others went to Norway and Sweden (m/1893 and M/1887 respectively), Serbia, Brazil and possibly Argentina.

In the early 1890s the Nagants patented a 'gas-seal' design in which the cylinder was cammed forward over the barrel to minimize the escape of gas at the cylinder/barrel joint. This was hardly novel, being found on the Collier revolvers made in the early 1820s, claimed in a U.S. patent in the 1830s and incorporated in an 1886 Pieper design, and it is debatable if the requisite mechanical complexity was worth the comparatively meagre gains.

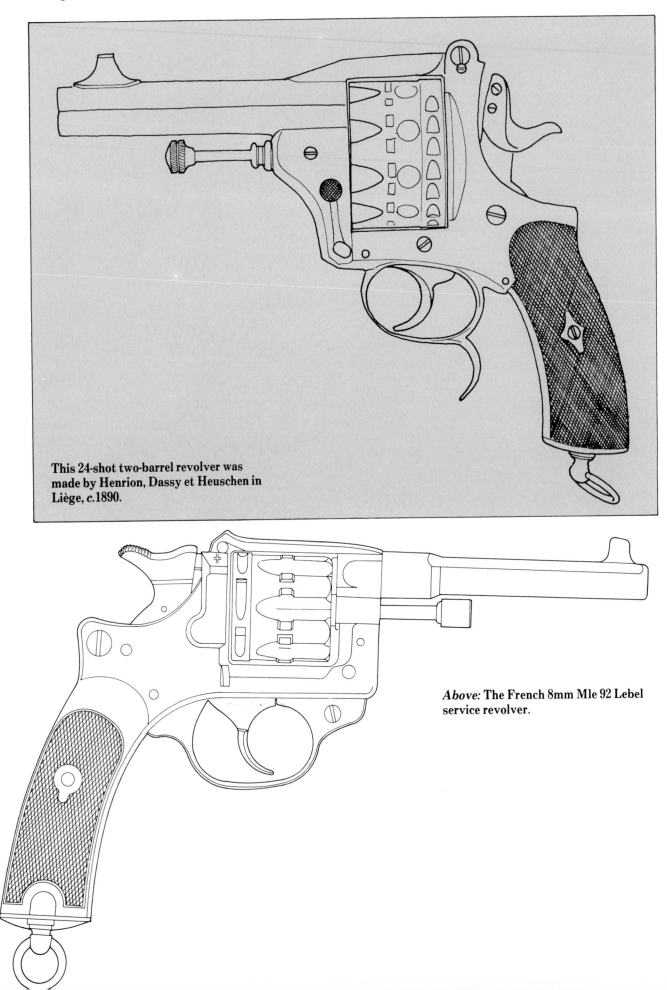

This 24-shot two-barrel revolver was made by Henrion, Dassy et Heuschen in Liège, *c*.1890.

Above: **The French 8mm Mle 92 Lebel service revolver.**

The Austrian 8mm M1898 revolver.

Nevertheless, the Nagant system so impressed the Russians that large numbers of obr.1895g revolvers were made until at least 1944. The incorporation of the gas-seal in a modern target revolver indicates the regard in which the principle is still held in the Soviet Union.

By the 1890s, France, Germany and Switzerland had combined elements of several differing designs in their service revolvers. Germany had assembled an ill-assorted collection of features into the clumsy, almost unbelievably basic 10.6mm Reichsrevolver of 1879, despite the existence of Mauser's appreciably better designed Model 1878 or 'Zig Zag' revolver and its solid-frame military counterpart. Switzerland's service revolver, Ordonnanz 1882, was the precise opposite of the Reichsrevolver: small, neat, beautifully made and very elegant, but firing an ineffectual 7.5mm-calibre cartridge. The French 8mm Revolver d'Ordonnance Mle.92, generally known as the 'Lebel' after the chairman of the trials commission, was really a combination of the earlier Mle.73 (Chamelot-Delvigne) and laterally swinging cylinder based on contemporary American practice. However, the Lebel's cylinder swung out to the right of the frame. Consequently, most firers had to transfer the gun to the non-firing hand to load it.

The contemporary European commercial market was satisfied by the output of large numbers of similar-looking pocket revolvers made by companies such as Auguste Francotte et Cie, Henrion, Dassy et Heuschen of Liége ('HDH') and Friedrich Pickert of Zella St Blasii, whose products usually bore the 'Arminius' brandname. In Britain, Webley made large numbers of .32 and .38 pocket and general-purpose revolvers, while cheap Smith & Wesson copies emanated from Spain.

6. A False Dawn

If something can go wrong, it will . . .

Murphy's Law (apocryphal)

No sooner had the revolver been improved to a point where it was suited to mass production than inventors began to seek its peer. We can now only marvel at the fertile imagination that produced the most ingenious of the revolver's rivals, the repeating pistol. Very few of these had any lasting effect on handgun design, however, and – almost without exception – have disappeared on the scrap-heap of history.

There are several differing classes, from which, for this book at least, pepperboxes and revolvers have been excluded. Manually operated turret guns and chain repeaters have already been discussed in Chapter 3.

Mechanically-actuated turret guns are very rare, the only important example being the 'Protector', patented in the U.S.A. by the Parisian Jacques-Edmond Turbiaux in March 1883. The cartridges were loaded into the cylinder through the removable side-plate; a spring-loaded trigger at the rear of the mechanism was squeezed to rotate the cylinder, cock and release the firing pin. The barrel protruded between the second and third finger allowing the trigger to be squeezed with the heel of the palm. Made by the Ames Sword Company, .32 seven-shot Protectors are usually marked as the products of the Chicago or Minneapolis Fire Arms Companies. 8mm-calibre examples were made in France.

Among the best known mechanical repeaters is the Volcanic, developed in the mid nineteenth century. Its origins lay in patents granted to Walter Hunt of New York in 1848-9 to protect a phenomenally complicated repeating rifle and the 'Volition Ball' – a bullet which, anticipating the rocket cartridges of the twentieth century, contained its own propellant. The project interested a New York financier named George Arrowsmith, who retained gunsmith Lewis Jennings to improving the Hunt rifle. Jennings received a patent on Christmas Day 1849, but the entire project was then sold to Courtlandt Palmer for $100,000. Palmer contracted for 5,000 Jennings-type rifles with Robbins & Lawrence, where he first came into contact with Horace Smith.

Despite Smith's 1851 patent of improvement, the Jennings rifle proved a disappointment. By 1854, however, Horace Smith and Edwin Wesson had patented an improved cartridge and a magazine pistol, and production of the latter – and an occasional carbine –

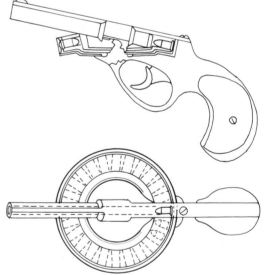

Trippett's was one of the last turret repeaters; American, 1899.

**The American Volcanic repeater was
one of the first pistol-size mechanical
repeaters.**

began immediately. Financed by Palmer, Smith & Wesson made
about 1,700 .31 pocket and .41 large-frame pistols in a workshop in
Norwich, Connecticut. Unhappily, the guns were comparatively
expensive, low powered and inaccurate, and the fulminate powder
charge was very corrosive. In 1855, the partners sold out to the
Volcanic Arms Company of New Haven, Connecticut; Wesson was
retained as works superintendent while Smith left, disillusioned.
The Volcanic pistols were made in two calibres – .31 and .39, known
as 'No.1' and 'No.2' respectively – and three differing barrel
lengths. The larger-calibre guns fired a 100-grain ball with 6½
grains of black powder, the original fulminate powder being
abandoned after spontaneous ignition blew the magazine off too
frequently.

The Volcanic Arms Company was declared insolvent in 1857, its
assets being acquired by Oliver Winchester and transferred to the
New Haven Arms Company. Eventually, the limitations of the
Volcanic ball were realised, a rimfire cartridge substituted by
Benjamin Henry and the ineffectual Volcanic became the desirable
Henry Rifle in 1860. The lever-action Henry subsequently developed
into the Winchester Model 1866.

The lever-action Volcanic pistol had a tube magazine under its
barrel. A ring-tipped lever, forming the trigger guard, fed the
projectile into the breech each time the action was operated.
However, this was still essentially a two-hand operation even
though the Volcanic anticipated the 'one-hand' European designs of
the 1880s in many other respects. Unfortunately, the principal
advantages of the Volcanic, not least of which was its large
magazine capacity, were all but negated by the curious ammunition;
and the guns, which were quite promising, remained curios despite
the efforts of its manufacturers to conjure up impressive-sounding
(but undoubtedly fraudulent) testimonials. The repeating pistol soon

passed from the American scene, leaving the concept of the Hunt-type self-contained ammunition to be explored much more recently in the MBA Gyrojet project (with, it must be said, a similar lack of success).

By the 1870s, the European revolver, like its American cousin, was well established. However, the European enthusiast, unlike his American equivalent blazing his new frontier, often found time on his hands. It was the earnest hope of many an under-employed European gunsmith/inventor – as many a patent will testify – to discover a means not only of carving a niche in history but also making a fortune through something truly revolutionary. Many men in the 1870-85 period sought a gun that could be loaded, cocked and then fired with one hand.

It could not be a revolver: that had already been done. So the central Europeans eventually perfected the mechanical repeater, though whether 'perfected' may be applied to something so inefficient is debatable. What does seem reasonable, however, is to credit most of the early guns to the 'Bohemian School': the area of Austria-Hungary, as it then was, from which most of the inventors hailed. Only Mauser, who in 1886 toyed with a Volcanic-like lever-action repeater of stupefying complexity, remained outside this group. Belgian inventors such as Colnot worked in Liége, but their experimentation seems to have been confined to 1886-90 and, like Mauser, they were probably inspired by the production of Schülhof repeaters in Liége earlier in the 1880s.

The rotary bolts of Bohemian School repeaters, adapted from contemporary rifle practice, operate through a ring lever surrounding the trigger. Claims to novelty generally arise only from the magazine, safety and lockwork arrangements, but research is still needed to determine the sources of influence; Erwin Reiger's British Patent of 1889, for example, illustrates a detachable rotary magazine suspiciously similar to that patented by Karel Krnka a year previously . . . and then credits the remainder of the 'Reiger' gun to Passler & Seidl. And is the Bittner, notwithstanding its clip-loaded magazine and PATENT BITTNER markings, really a Reiger (i.e. a Passler & Seidl with a Reiger magazine) made by Bittner in his Weipert factory?

All these guns share a finger-lever operating system in which forward movement of the fingers of the firing hand unlock the bolt, move it backwards and then return the bolt to lock, stripping a round out of the magazine and into the breech on the rearward movement of the fingers. Many of the guns were designed for 'rapid fire' when the returning finger lever, with the index finger inserted in its aperture, automatically released the firing pin. They are very well made, if rather complicated, and operating the firing cycle is not as awkward or tiring as the foregoing description may suggest. The repeaters would have worked reasonably well had they been new, clean, well lubricated and firing good quality ammunition. However, there is little primary extraction, and a troublesome or sticky cartridge case would undoubtedly have required the strength of both hands to complete the extraction/ejection cycle.

The Laumann repeater of 1890-1 (*right*) and the Mauser-Repetierpistole C/86 (*left*) were among the European oddities.

The 'squeezers' included the Gaulois, the Little All Right, the Rouchouse (sic), the Tribuzio and the Unique. Apart from the Unique, all used pistol-like magazines in the gun-body and relied on a squeezing action to chamber, fire, extract and eject each cartridge. The five-shot 8mm Gaulois has its squeeze-grip at the rear of an especially flat body, and features a radial safety catch on the body-side. The Rouchouse (probably meant for 'Roughhouse') is similar, but has a fixed body with the squeezer at the front; both it and the Gaulois are French. The Little All Right, made by the Little All Right Fire Arms Company of Lawrence, Massachusetts, to the patent of Edward Boardman & Andrew Peavey (January 1876) is a five-shot .22 rimfire revolver with a sliding trigger above the barrel housing. It is held in the hand with the vestigial butt against the palm-heel and the muzzle protruding between the index and first fingers, whereafter the index finger can retract the trigger-slide. The Tribuzio, invented by Catello Tribuzio of Turin about 1890, is similar to the Gaulois but is shaped to accommodate the thumb-web and its forward-pointing trigger ring is retracted by the third finger of the firing hand. The Unique, made by C.S. Shattuck of Hatfield, Massachusetts, to the 1900 patent of Oscar Mossberg, has four fixed barrels fired in turn by a squeezer-actuated rotating striker.

The rapid emergence of the truly semi-automatic pistol at the end of the period in which the repeating guns were being perfected swept them all away. The big-bore repeaters could never hope to compete with even the most primitive of the early automatics, and only the small 'palm squeezers' enjoyed a brief and rather irrational heyday.

Few of the early repeaters, however, could compare in complexity and grand intent with the clockwork-powered revolving cylinder rifle designed by Georg Bunsen in the 1860s. This delights the student of automata greater than the seeker of firearms efficiency; it may be presumed to have worked – several patent models are known – but the integral power system had no future: if any parts of the horribly complex mechanism broke, the gun would grind to a halt!

7. A New Dawn

The naval small arms board had exhibited before it today a pistol which is quite likely to revolutionize this sort of equipment in the armies and navies of the world . . .

From a report of Borchardt pistol trials in the *Boston Herald*, 22 November 1894

Controversy surrounds the first appearance of the true semi-automatic pistol and the influence, if any, exerted by the perfected mechanical repeaters on its design. This is not helped by the inability of modern researchers to agree on the dating of the earliest designs, or unravel the many claims.

Though Hiram Maxim claimed to have invented a pistol in the 1880s, the most plausible claimants are the French Clair brothers, Benoït, Jean-Baptiste and Victor. Their pistol was a huge, unwieldy diminutive of the 'Clair-Eclair' gas-operated shotgun dating, so the French say, to 1885-9. Naturally, this has been strongly disputed and the only relevant British patent, which dates from 1893, is often cited to 'discredit' the Clairs' claim; however, a pistol had been submitted to the French Army in 1888 along with a semi-automatic rifle. As the French introduced the first military smallbore cartridge loaded with semi-smokeless propellant, and as the Clair-Eclair was being marketed commercially by 1890-1, the brothers Clair probably deserve a lion's share of the credit.

But the Clair pistol was a commercial flop. Other early pistols include an otherwise obscure long-recoil design by the Hungarian Otto Brauswetter, acquired by Theodor Bergmann to be transformed into the delayed blowback Bergmann-Schmeisser and then into a simple blowback. A more popular 'first successful automatic' claimant is Laumann's, derived from mechanical repeaters patented in 1890-2 and generally known as the Schönberger. Judging by the patents, the Laumann/Schönberger pistol incorporates a form of hesitation lock, though some researchers have claimed it to be from the ultra-rare primer-projection group. The absence of any authenticated 8mm Schönberger cartridge – in itself, very significant – still makes the 'primer projection' theory marginally tenable.

The Laumann/Schönberger, an adaptation of the inventor's earlier mechanical repeaters, supports a popular belief that the great leap from mechanical actuation to automaticity was no more than simple progression. However, as Maxim had been experimenting with recoil-operated machine-guns in the early 1880s, the basis for autoloading dated from the *beginning* of the brief

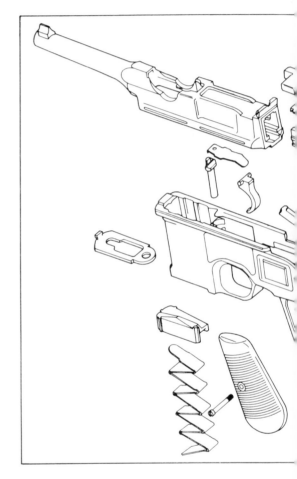

The pieces of the Mauser C/96 interlocked without requiring screws.

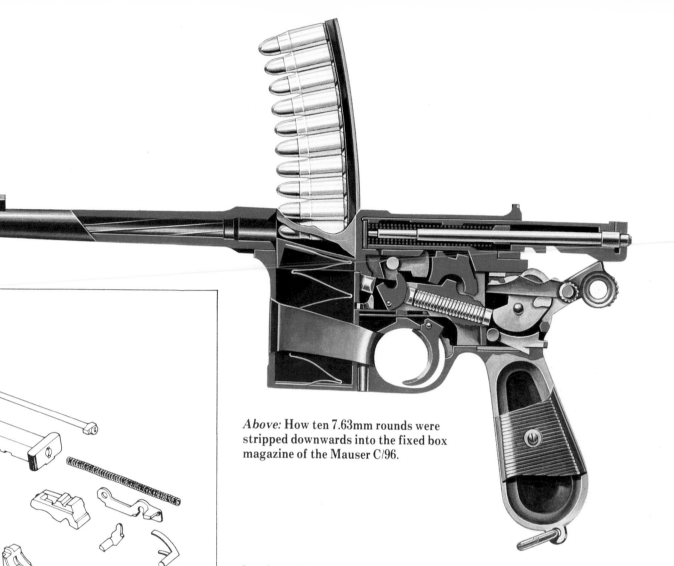

Above: How ten 7.63mm rounds were stripped downwards into the fixed box magazine of the Mauser C/96.

heyday of the mechanical repeaters and the two should be considered as contemporaries.

Laumann filed the first Laumann/Schönberger pistol patent in France in March 1892, which makes the pistol important chronologically; but to claim it as the first commercially successful design, as many writers have done, is unreasonable. The survivors are all numbered below ten; should it simply be assumed that only a handful of these elegant, well balanced guns was made for the Austrian army trials held in 1894-5 – and that the inflated modern reputation is entirely due to prompt retirement to military study collections?

On the heels of the Schönberger came more effectual designs, some of whose origins may eventually prove to pre-date Laumann's final patent by several years. The Borchardt pistol – patented in Germany in 1893 – probably deserves to be recognised as the first truly successful semi-automatic, though all too soon overshadowed by the Mauser C/96 and the perfected Borchardt-Luger.

The Borchardt relied on recoil sliding the barrel/receiver unit backward over the frame. The breech comprised a knee-like toggle joint, locked solid at rest, which could be broken by a slight-but-perceptible movement of a roller inside the closed rear frame. The breechblock was drawn back from the breech face as the toggle-joint

broke upward, until, at the end of the opening stroke, a helical riband spring in a housing below the back of the frame propelled the breechblock back up to the breech face. During this closing stroke, a fresh cartridge was stripped out of the magazine and the 'knee' portion of the toggle-joint finally fell below the longitudinal axis of the barrel. Forces developing back through the base of the cartridge thereafter forced the knee downwards against the solid metal of the receiver and prevented the breech opening until the whole unit had slid back far enough for the chamber pressure to decay.

Born in Germany in the early 1850s, Hugo Borchardt had arrived in the U.S.A. with his parents during the great emigrations from

Above: **A 7.65mm Borchardt C/93 with the toggle open. This was the first successful semi-automatic.**

Below: **The Borchardt C/93, its magazine and screwdriver.**

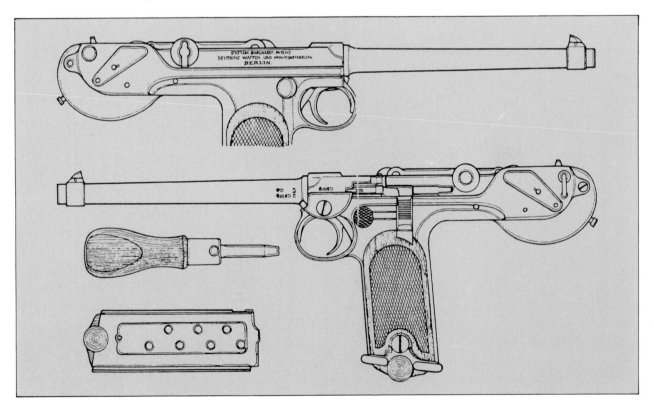

Europe immediately after the end of the American Civil War. Work for Sharps and Winchester soon showed that Borchardt was a supremely talented engineer. He even became a U.S. citizen in the 1870s (allowing the improbable claim that his pistol is 'a U.S. design'), but was disillusioned by Winchester's failure to exploit his revolver and returned to Europe to work at the Hungarian State firearms factory. Circumstantial evidence suggests that prototype pistols had been readied by 1891-92, and the drawings accompanying the first German patent certainly show several non-standard features. Borchardt even approached Fabrique Nationale d'Armes de Guerre but reportedly stormed out in a huff after his pistol had been rejected as unsalesworthy.

Small-scale production then began in the Berlin factory of Ludwig Loewe & Co., a prosperous sewing-machine maker with substantial shareholding in Waffenfabrik Mauser as well as appreciable previous gunmaking experience. Sufficient components were made for about 3,000 Borchardt pistols, though many were subsequently assembled and marked by Deutsche Waffen- und Munitionsfabriken, a post-1896 partnership between Loewe and Germany's premier ammunition maker, Deutsche Metallpatronenfabrik. The first pistols are believed to have reached the market in the autumn of 1894, but substantiation is still lacking.

Though the C/93 had several severe disadvantages, it could operate very well when properly adjusted; in the 1897 U.S. Army trials, there were only four jams in more than 2,000 shots. However, the helical mainspring was capricious and the guns worked only when adjusted to specific batches of cartridges. Smokeless propellant technology was in its infancy in the mid 1890s, and pressures could vary appreciably. As the tension in the Borchardt mainspring was difficult to regulate without gunsmiths' tools, the commercial pistols rarely shot as well as the specially selected trial guns. The excessive rear overhang of the receiver and the mainspring housing contributed greatly to poor balance, though the Borchardt made a passable light semi-automatic carbine when fitted with its sturdy shoulder stock; but it was conceived as a pistol, and as a pistol it was judged.

Subsequent events relegated the Borchardt to comparative obscurity and have rather stolen its claim to be not only the first commercially successful semi-automatic pistol but also the first to convince sceptical military agencies that such guns had a future. Unfortunately, Loewe then granted Mauser use of the C/93 cartridge as part of a supposedly mutually beneficial exchange of ideas; Borchardt, reportedly, was furious.

Whether Mauser had a gun in mind at this time may be questionable, but one was soon found. Despite being patented in Mauser's name in December 1895, it was the work of the three Feederle brothers. It is popularly believed that the design was nearly complete when the Borchardt pistol appeared; disparities in timescale, however, suggest that Mauser obtained rights to the cartridge in the summer of 1894, cast around for a gun, and the Feederles *then* came forward with a vague notion that was perfected around the Borchardt cartridge. No prototype (or even drawing) chambering anything other than the 7.63mm Mauser cartridge has yet been produced.

The prototype Mauser pistol was fired – possibly for the first time – in March 1895. Christened 'C/96', it appeared on the market in 1896; one was even test-fired by Kaiser Wilhelm II, which did no harm to its chances of success. Mauser had access to the highest levels of German society and held an important social advantage over Borchardt.

The C/96 was operated on short recoil principles, as had been the Borchardt, but a sturdy block pivoting beneath the breech replaced the delicate toggle. Thus the Mauser action was more secure than the Borchardt's, particularly on the closing stroke where the toggle system possessed little residual energy. It was also beautifully made, the parts interlocking without so much as a screw. As a piece of engineering, the Mauser was a triumph; but it was too complicated to be produced cheaply – a recurring problem with

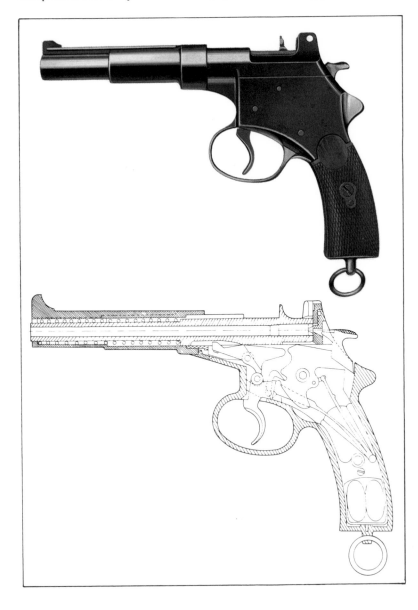

Left: The 7.6mm-calibre Mannlicher blow-forward pistol of 1894.

The .45-calibre Gabbett-Fairfax 'Mars' pistol at full recoil.

7.65mm 1900-pattern Borchardt-Luger number '01' was delivered to the Swiss army in 1901.

German pistols – and was initially very susceptible to jamming. Many of its present-day champions gloss over this flaw, relying more on factory-staged endurance trials than the hostile reports of contemporary military trials in Germany or Britain (55 jams in 180 rounds in the latter). Violent cycling tended to push the bullets back into the casemouth if they were too loosely crimped-in, and the feedway was a little too steep. However, these faults were soon corrected and the Mauser remained in production into the 1930s.

Sales of the C/96 were boosted by war in South Africa (1899-1902), the Russo-Japanese War (1904-5) and the unrest in Russia that ended in revolution in 1905. Surviving sales figures show these boom periods most clearly; Winston Churchill was among the most famous users of the C/96 in South Africa. Yet military acceptance still eluded Mauser. A few guns had been acquired by the Italian navy in 1899 – the first European military agency to adopt a semi-automatic pistol – but most testers remained unconvinced. This does not infer that guns received unfair treatment; the Germans and British, for instance, paid near-fanatical attention to each new design. Guns simply never performed as efficiently before trial boards as in their makers' factories; and delicate construction was cruelly exposed in dust, sand and rusting tests.

The Mauser pistol had a similar-looking contemporary, patented by Ferdinand von Mannlicher in 1896. Mannlicher is reckoned among giants of firearms history, but his various pistols were collectively most uninspiring: the oldest, generally known as the Model 1894, featured a blow-forward system; one of two 1896 patents protected a fragile blowback; and only the last, an elegant blowback patented in Germany in 1898, achieved tangible success with perhaps 10,000 sales prior to 1914. The Mauser-like pistol, briefly revived in the twentieth century as the 'Model 1903', was locked by a weak propped-up strut rather than a sturdy pivoting block. Unfortunately, the powerful Mauser cartridge could also chamber and fire in the Model 1903, courting disaster as the latter

107

was not strong enough to take the extra pressure.

The Mauser C/96 also appears to have inspired Kijiro Nambu, whose autobiography claims that experimentation dated back to the '30th Year Automatic Pistol Plan' of 1897; by 1902, he had perfected the 8mm Nambu Shiki Jidō Ken-jū ('Nambu-type self-acting pistol') by combining the pivoting locking block of the C/96 with the box magazine and general lines of the Borchardt-Luger. Uniquely, the coil-pattern mainspring lies in a separate chamber on the left side of the bolt. About 2,500 pistols, distinguished by their extraordinarily small trigger guards, were made by the Tokyo Artillery Arsenal between c.1903 and 1906. A modified pattern was then made by the arsenal and the Tokyo Gas & Electric Company, some being purchased by the Imperial Japanese Navy during World War I. A 7mm-calibre diminutive was also produced in small numbers.

Dating the Nambu to the first years of the twentieth century proves that it was copied neither from the Swiss Häussler-Roch pistol, patented in 1903, nor the Italian Glisenti (1906-7) – all of which derived directly from the C/96, their similarity being coincidental.

The most influential of the powerful semi-automatic pistols being touted in 1900 was the Borchardt-Luger. This had been derived from the Borchardt, by way of several intermediaries before the submission of a perfected gun to the Swiss army in 1899. The Borchardt-Luger incorporated a toggle system comparable with that of the C/93, expecting that the helical riband spring in the rear of the frame became a leaf-spring in the back of the grip behind the magazine. Cam-ramps on the frame deflected the toggle 'knee' upward as recoil drove the barrel and receiver backward. Though still largely Borchardt in concept, the changes resulted in a neater, handier and lighter gun.

The Swiss army adopted the 7.65mm-calibre Borchardt-Luger in May 1900. Similar guns underwent searching U.S. Army examination – 1,000 being acquired for troop trials – and in Britain, where a submission was received most favourably. Unfortunately, 7.65mm (.30in) was much too small to be an effectual man-stopper by the standards of the British .455 revolver cartridge and the Parabellum was rejected. Though a 9mm gun was proffered in 1903 – its first recorded appearance – the British army had turned instead to the 'Mars' pistol.

The Mars was the brainchild of Hugh Gabbett-Fairfax, who, according to the Birmingham Daily Post (4 February 1899), had approached Webley in May 1898. Impressed, Webley had agreed to make prototypes for the Mars Automatic Pistol Syndicate. Gabbett-Fairfax's Mars was the biggest and most powerful semi-automatic pistol of its era, its characteristics anticipating the later British Small Arms Committee requirements for a 200-grain bullet travelling at 1,200 feet per second. Design work is said to have begun in 1895, but it is doubtful if much progress had been made prior to the first approach to Webley. Made in several differing calibres, including 8.5mm, .360 (or 9mm) and at least two .45 patterns, the Mars allied long-recoil operation and great complexity

A typical Webley .38 automatic pistol.

with a unique breech system. When the gun fired, the barrel, receiver and breechblock assembly retreated to the end of a very long stroke. The breechblock was then rotated out of engagement with the remainder of the parts, which immediately returned to their original position. The extractor pulled the spent case from the barrel as the latter ran forward; when the barrel stopped, the ejector kicked the spent case clear of the gun and the breechblock could then return to strip a new round from the cartridge lifter and lock the mechanism for the next shot.

Apart from prodigious weight, the Mars suffered a major disadvantage; the weight of the moving parts – and the distance they travelled – was such that even experienced firers could not control recoil and the muzzle ended up pointing skywards after each shot. Conscious effort was required to drag it back down again. After one particularly exasperating trial, the Captain of HMS *Excellent*, the Royal Navy's gunnery school, reported that 'no one who had fired . . . [the Mars] . . . wished to do so again.' It seems curious that the British dallied with it for so long.

Webley soon became disillusioned with the Mars, preferring to keep future developments within the company. After a series of experimental guns patented in 1903-6, the Whiting-designed .25 pocket and .32 police-model external hammer semi-automatic pistols appeared in 1906. These were supplemented by a .380-calibre version (1908), a hammerless .25 and a 9mm hammer model in 1909, and .38 HV hammerless models in 1910 and 1913. In 1911, the .32 Webley received an unexpected boost from the infamous Siege of Sydney Street, where a band of anarchists led by Peter the Painter had killed three policemen before the Home Secretary – Winston Churchill – had called in the Scots Guards. The subsequent enquiry recommended the issue of pistols to the Metropolitan Police, the Webley being selected. Where the Metropolitan led, other forces followed; some guns were even made under licence in the U.S.A. by Harrington & Richardson.

While the British Army toyed with the Mars, the Germans finally accepted the Borchardt-Luger at the expense of the Mauser C/96. The German navy accepted the army's advice and placed the first contracts for a 9mm Parabellum in December 1904. Though the army was determined to follow, Mauser blocked adoption of his arch-rival long enough for an assortment of his 'improved' pistols to be submitted. None of these proved effectual enough and, after a few hundred New Model Parabellums had been purchased for machine-gun detachments in 1906-7, a version without a grip safety was adopted on 22 August 1908 as the '9mm Selbstladepistole 1908'. Issues began in 1909.

Adoption in Germany restricted commercial sales of the Parabellum, benefiting Mauser just as Colt had gained from Smith & Wesson's Russian contract in the early 1870s (see Chapter 5). While Mauser and DWM – makers of the C/96 and Parabellum respectively – strove to outwit and outsell each other, lesser

The German LP08 ('Artillery Luger') Luger was issued with a holster-stock and – in World War I – a special 32-round 'snail' magazine.

inventors sought toeholds in the market. In Europe, there were many near-successes. These included the smallest-calibre locked-breech pistol ever mass-produced. Designed by Ignacio Charola and Juan Anitua of Eibar in 1897, about 5,000 5mm and 7mm-calibre guns were made by Charola y Anitua and its successor, I. Charola y Cia, from 1898 until about 1910.

The Fosbery Auto-Revolver was another eccentric design. Patented by Colonel George Fosbery VC in 1895-6, about 3,500 guns were made by the Webley & Scott Revolver & Arms Company Ltd (pre-1906 examples) and its successor, Webley & Scott Ltd. Recoil rotated the zig-zag grooved cylinder and cocked the hammer. First demonstrated at the Imperial Meeting, Bisley, in 1900, the .38 or .455 Webley-Fosbery was made in several barrel lengths, proving popular for target shooting until its unusually soft or 'cushioned' recoil led to a ban from revolver competitions. It fascinated the U.S. Army trials board of 1907 before being rejected; and was made

The 'New Model' Parabellum, developed in 1904, had a coil-type mainspring.

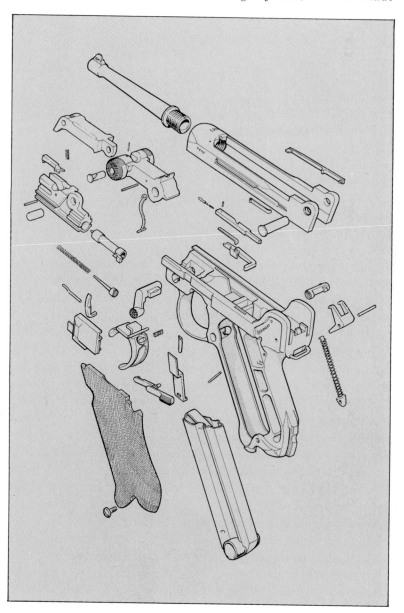

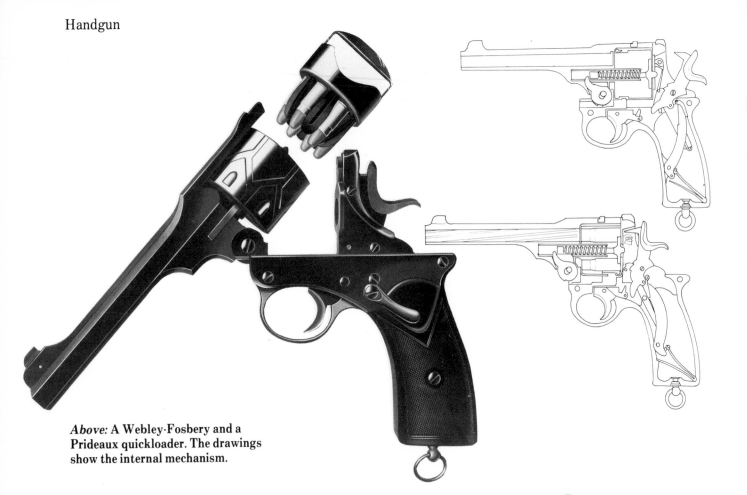

Above: **A Webley-Fosbery and a Prideaux quickloader. The drawings show the internal mechanism.**

under licence by the Union Arms Company, active in Toledo, Ohio, in 1907-13. But it proved to be sensitive to mud, and a tight grip was needed to ensure that recoil revolved the cylinder properly. Consequently, the Fosbery Auto-Revolver had been abandoned by 1914.

After some aberrant experiments, Andreas Schwarzlose developed an effectual 9mm 'Standart' pistol in 1898. However, sales of the Schwarzlose were so poor that many remained in store into the twentieth century, to be purchased at a knock-down price by the 1905 revolutionaries and shipped back to Russia. Production is estimated at no greater than a thousand guns, which was miniscule compared with the output of Fabrique Nationale (100,000 FN-Brownings by 4 August 1904), Mauser (46,509 C/96 pistols by the end of 1905) and DWM (about 30,000 Parabellums in the same period). The Standart was a good design for its time, lacking only a reliable ejector, and failed more through its manufacturer's weakness than any inherent design flaws. Schwarzlose, inspired by the adoption of his machine-gun by the Austro-Hungarian armies, then produced a few thousand Model 1908 pistols before World War I began, making it the most successful of guns in which the barrel is projected forward from the breech at the instant of firing.

The Bergmanns fared rather differently. Louis Schmeisser was a talented if somewhat eccentric designer, typical of the oddity of his early work being the 'blow-out' ejectorless cartridge expulsion system found on many pre-1900 pocket pistols. None of Schmeisser's

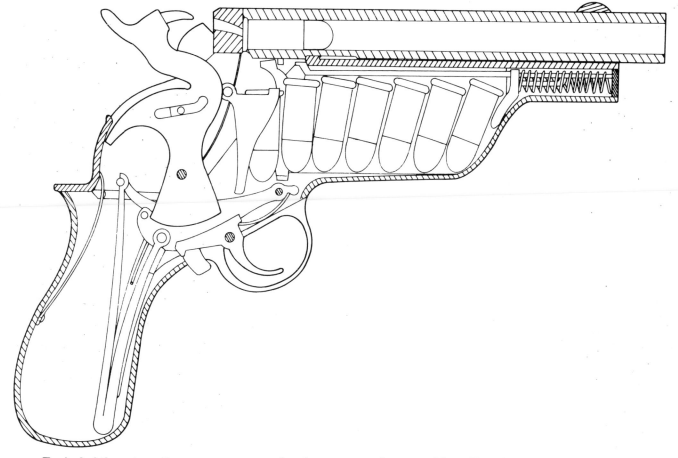

Typical of the extraordinary Schwarzlose designs was this 1892-vintage effort.

handguns proved acceptable militarily until the advent of the Bergmann-Mars (not to be confused with the Gabbett-Fairfax Mars) in 1902. As so much of Bergmann's fame rests on his role as an exploiter of others' ideas, it is ironic that, just as the Mars had been adopted by the Spanish Army, the production arrangement between Bergmann and V.C. Schilling & Co. was terminated when the latter was acquired by Krieghoff.

Bergmann finally had the success he craved, but no means of producing it; his pocket pistols disappeared and the Mars, licensed to Anciens Etablissements Pieper of Liége in 1908, was renamed 'Bergmann-Bayard' after Pieper's trademark. It was adopted by Denmark and (probably) Greece prior to 1914, while several thousand were supplied to Spain to replace worn-out Bergmann-Mars Mo.1903. Elsewhere, however, the Mars encountered little success: it was somewhat clumsy and prone to jamming. In the U.S. Army trials of 1906-7, .45 ammunition was confiscated by the U.S. Customs and the Mars did not receive a fair trial; but it seems that even the Danes would have adopted the Parabellum had DWM been willing to grant a production licence.

While Schwarzlose, Bergmann and Schmeisser were struggling, the American John Moses Browning produced his first semi-automatic pistols. Browning's earliest firearms dated from the late 1860s, and his dropping-block action rifle had been commercially exploited by Winchester in the 1870s. By the end of the century, with many firearms patents to his name, he had perfected the

Top: The 6.5mm Bergmann Nr.3, 1896.

Above, left: The Bergmann-Simplex, *c.*1904-10.

Winchester lever-action repeater (the Model 1894 remaining in production even today) and developed the 'potato digger' machine-gun for Colt. In 1897, Browning filed four differing pistol designs with the U.S. Patent Office and one of the greatest triumphs in handgun history had begun. Two pistols were abandoned after no more than a prototype of each had been made. The third, a small blowback, was offered to and rather surprisingly rejected by Colt; however, it was then offered to Fabrique Nationale d'Armes de Guerre by Hart O. Berg, Colt's European representative, and production rights were negotiated. In Europe, excepting Britain, small calibres and low power were not the inhibition to sales they may have been in the Wild West.

The Mle.1900 FN-Browning blowback was adopted in Belgium and sold commercially in huge quantities. Its improved successor, the 'Grande Modèle' or Mle.1903, was then made under licence by Colt – who, having declined Browning's initial approaches, made about 775,000 .32 and .380 blowback pistols. The FN-Browning Mle.1903 was adopted in Belgium, The Netherlands, Sweden (as the M/07), Russia, Turkey, Paraguay and elsewhere. Next came a tiny pocket pistol, the 6.35mm-calibre Mle.1906 made by FN and Colt, and then the sleek-looking Mle.1910 pocket pistol chambering the 7.65 or 9mm Short cartridges (.32 and .380 ACP). On 31 January 1914, FN presented the millionth FN-Browning pistol, a Modèle 1906, to John Browning.

The Spanish Victoria was copied from the 6.35mm-calibre FN-Browning pistol of 1906.

An engraved .32 ACP M1903 Colt.

Browning's second successful 1897 patent protected the 'parallel ruler' system. When the pistol fired, recoil moved the slide and barrel backward while still securely locked together; once pressure in the system had dropped sufficiently, the links, rotated by the rearward movement of the slide, began to pull the barrel down until its lugs disengaged corresponding locking recesses in the inner top surface of the slide. The barrel block stopped against the frame, allowing the slide to run back alone to the limit of its travel; the coil-type mainspring then pushed the barrel forwards again, stripping a new cartridge out of the magazine and raising the barrel lugs into the slide recesses. The guns were not only simple and amazingly durable, but also very efficient. Colt approached the U.S. Army and trials began. The pistols proceeded through various models – 1900, 1902 and 1905 – until, in the trials of 1906-7, the Colt-Browning comprehensively beat the Parabellum, the Savage and a handful of lesser designs.

Though the U.S. Army subconsciously biased the trials in favour of the Colt-Browning by adopting a Colt-Browning cartridge (the Parabellum and the Savage being effectively brand-new and untried

The 7.65mm FN-Browning Mle 1900 was the first truly successful blowback pistol.

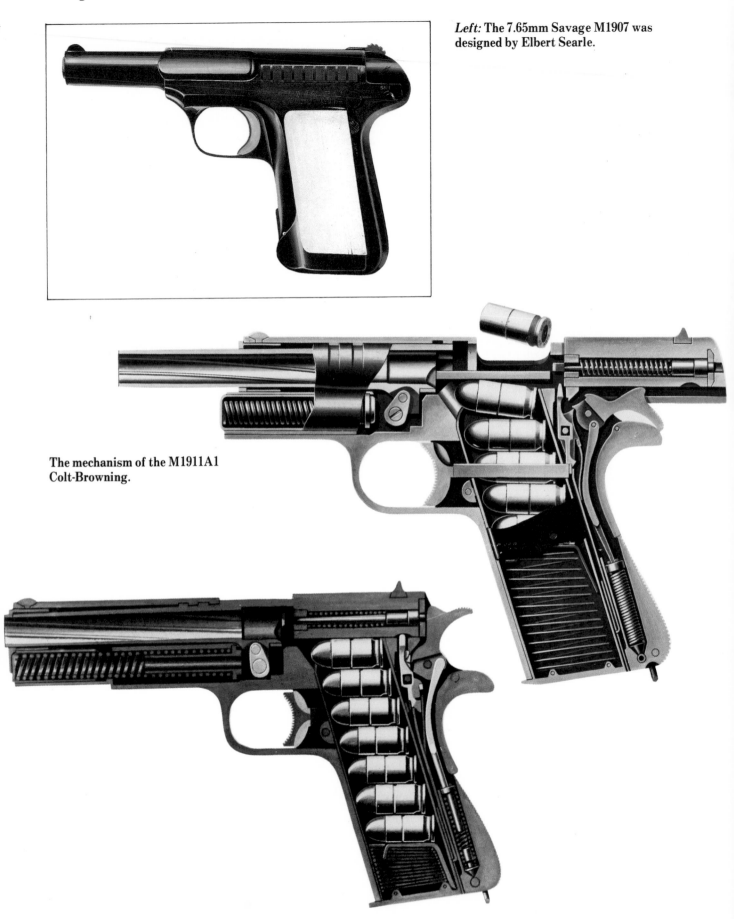

Left: The 7.65mm Savage M1907 was
designed by Elbert Searle.

The mechanism of the M1911A1
Colt-Browning.

designs), there can be no doubting the Browning system's strength and efficacy. The Parabellum always proved more accurate, owing to its axial barrel movement, but was never as reliable; the weakness of its breech-closing stroke was usually exposed in rust and dust tests.

In 1909, Browning patented an improved breech-locking system with only a single pivot at the breech, the muzzle being supported in the slide-mouth. Compared with the earlier parallel-ruler system – and especially the Parabellum – accuracy suffered, but the simplified construction improved durability even more. One Model 1909 Colt-Browning underwent an endurance trial in which 6,000 rounds were fired without a single malfunction attributable to the gun and, on 29 March 1911, the perfected pistol was finally adopted by the U.S. Army. An order for 31,344 guns went to Colt on 5 May 1911, and a licence was negotiated to allow production to begin in Springfield Armory once 50,000 pistols had been ordered.

The 'Government Model' Browning gave Colt an important technical lead over the other U.S. manufacturers of automatic pistols. The Reifgraber, Harrington & Richardson's licence-built Webley and the Warner Infallible had all failed near-completely by 1920, and the first .35 Smith & Wesson was also encountering apathy (only 8,250 were made in 1913-22).

By the time the U.S. Army entered World War I in 1917, more than 75,000 M1911 pistols had been delivered by Colt and Springfield Armory; many others had gone to Russia and Britain for war service, and Norway, after buying some commercial guns as the 'm/1912', had negotiated a licence to make m/1914 pistols in the government manufactory in Kongsberg. As slightly modified Government Models are still being made by Colt, the basic 1911 Colt-Browning is still one of the few semi-automatic pistols to remain practically unchanged for more than seventy years.

8. And so to War

Weapons are an important factor in war, but not the decisive one; it is man and not materials that counts.

Mao Tse-Tung, 1938

In the mid-morning of 28 June 1914, a young Bosnian nationalist named Gavrilo Princip shot and fatally injured the heir to the Austrian throne, Archduke Franz Ferdinand, and his wife Sophie during a state visit to the Serbian capital Sarajevo. Within days, Europe was at war.

No one realised the extent to which the struggle would involve the armies of the world, or that the conflict would be especially lengthy. Moods were buoyant: the war, people said, would be over by Christmas. But 1914 dragged into 1915; and then into 1916; and then into another New Year with no end in sight. As the conflict escalated, more and more men were called to the colours. To arm them, ever-increasing numbers of guns were needed.

In August 1914, the regular armies of Austria-Hungary, Britain, France, Germany, Italy and Russia were well equipped, though some satellite armies were not so lucky: the Balkan War of 1912-13, for example, had taken a toll of the weapons of Greece, Bulgaria, Serbia, Romania and Turkey, and there had not been time to re-equip.

The two camps divided neatly into pro-revolver and pro-pistol. Although substantial quantities of revolvers were still in second-line service or held in reserve, German and Austro-Hungarian units generally carried pistols (the Parabellum in the former case, the Roth-Steyr in the latter's); the Allies, almost to a man, had revolvers such as the British Webley, the French Mle.92 'Lebel' and the Russian Nagant. The exception was Italy, in whose army the Mo.910 pistol ('Glisenti') jostled alongside the Mo.89 'Bodeo' revolver.

Most of these guns have already been discussed in the preceding chapters; it suffices to state that they were durable enough for military service and at least acceptably effectual. The German Pistole 1908, a Parabellum, was probably the best of the semi-automatics; the British Webley, with its powerful man-stopping .455-calibre cartridge and auto-ejection, was unquestionably the best of the revolvers.

The gunmaking industries, in Britain as in Germany, became increasingly incapable of supplying sufficient handguns to the vast new conscript armies as the war dragged on. An obvious stratagem was to accelerate production of the standard guns, recruiting extra contractors to assist. Virtually every country tried this first; but

The 9mm Austro-Hungarian Repetierpistole M 12 ('Steyr' or 'Steyr-Hahn').

The Repetierpistole M 7 or 'Roth-Steyr', designed specifically for cavalry use.

118

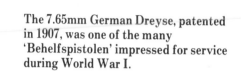

The 7.65mm German Dreyse, patented in 1907, was one of the many 'Behelfspistolen' impressed for service during World War I.

even with production running at full capacity, shortages of handguns were still evident. New solutions were needed.

Germany had the best semi-automatic pistol tradition prior to 1914; yet conversely, the worst revolvers. The pistols were Parabellums – the navy model of 1904, with a 15cm barrel and a two-position rocking-L back sight on the toggle-link; the army's Pistole 1908, with a 10cm barrel and fixed sights; and an 'artillery' model (actually developed for artillery drivers, machine-gunners, airmen and fortress artillery) with a 20cm barrel and a tangent-leaf sight on the barrel ahead of the receiver. By 1914, there were sufficient short-barrelled army guns to equip first-line troops; however, the enlargement of the navy meant that Pistolen 1904 were in short supply, and the Lange Pistole 08 had been adopted as recently as June 1913. Apart from accelerating Parabellum production and re-issuing the surviving commission revolvers of 1879 and 1883, the initial German reaction was to order as many serviceable pistols from the gun-trade as possible. In 1917, the Waffen- und Munitions-Beschaffungs-Amt reported that more than twenty pistols had been accepted for emergency service (as 'Behelfspistolen'), ranging from 6.35mm 'Lütticher Pistolen', simple blowbacks either made in occupied Liége or copied in Germany, to Mausers chambering the powerful 9mm 'Export' cartridge. How many of these guns were procured to bona fide military contracts is

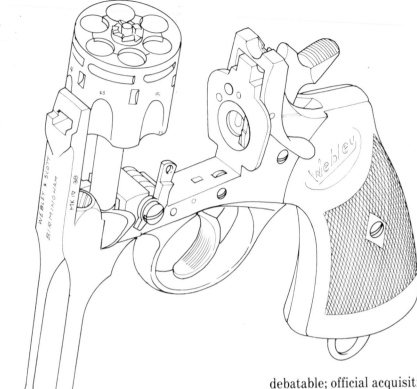

debatable; official acquisitions included the Mauser C/96 modified to chamber the standard 9mm Parabellum cartridge, together with the 7.65mm Dreyse, FL-Selbstlader, Jäger, Walther Modell 4 and the Beholla/Menta group. In addition, the Bavarian army acquired pistols from Austria-Hungary, and several experimental 9mm Parabellum derivatives of the 7.65mm-calibre blowbacks (e.g., the Dreyse and the Walther Modell 6) were developed specifically to army instructions.

The Mauser C/96 was undoubtedly the best Behelfspistole: the most powerful, eagerly sought and reckoned on a par with the LP08. 150,000 of the 9mm Parabellum version were ordered in 1916, at least 140,000 being delivered before the end of the war. Among the smaller guns, the Walther Modell 4 was particularly efficient; but the first FL-Selbstlader, made by Langenhan of Zella St. Blasii, was so poorly designed that the breechblock could fly out of the gun if its retaining screw loosened. A quirky 'locking system' could disengage when the 9mm Dreyse became worn, and continual battering of 9mm Parabellum ammunition proved too much for the blowback Walther Modell 6.

By November 1918, the Germans were better equipped with handguns than most other European armies. The Austro-Hungarians fared worse. In 1914, the regulation pistol had been the Repetierpistole M 7, designed by Karel Krnka and Georg Roth especially for the cavalry, and made in both Austria and Hungary. The standard M 98 revolver is now better known as the 'Rast & Gasser' after its original manufacturer, and the Hungarian reserve, the Honved, had the recoil-operated Frommer Pisztolý 12M. All three guns were solid and workmanlike, but there were too few of them to equip all the troops mobilised in 1914. Like Germany,

The Webley .38 Mark IV revolver.

Austria-Hungary promptly reissued obsolescent revolvers from store.

In 1911, however, Österreichische Waffenfabriks-Gesellschaft of Steyr, Austria's premier privately-owned smallarms manufacturer, had improved the Roth-Steyr. The new pistol was offered to the Austro-Hungarian armies, but was apparently still being tested when war began even though some had gone to Chile (navy) and Romania (army). A few had even been sold commercially. As the M 1911 Steyr pistol was clearly better than the older Roth-Steyr, it was pressed into service as the Repetierpistole M 12. Österreichische Waffenfabriks-Gesellschaft made about 275,000 during the period of hostilities. Curiously, though its own armies were desperately short of handguns, the Austrian government accepted two orders from the Bavarians – one in 1916 and the other in 1918 – which explains why M 12 pistols are occasionally found with the marks of Bavarian army corps or clothing depots. The only other pistol regularly used by the Austrian army appears to have

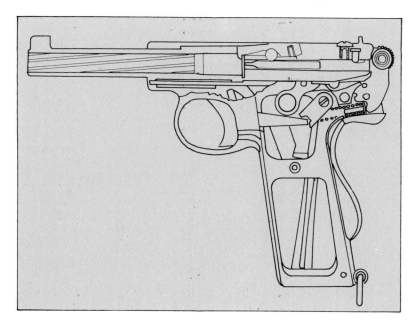

The .455-calibre Webley, designed by William Whiting, was tried and found wanting in the mud of the Western Front.

The Italian Mo.910 ('Glisenti') pistol.

been the 1909-model 7.65mm pocket pistol made by Steyr under licence from the Belgian Pieper company.

Of the other Central Powers, the Bulgarians had acquired 10,000 Parabellums shortly before the war began, differing from the Pistole 1908 only in markings and the provision of a lanyard ring on the butt-heel; Romania had small quantities of the 1911-model Austrian Steyr; and Turkey had 1903-model FN-Browning blowbacks. Each also had supplies of earlier weapons, usually Gasser- or Smith & Wesson-type revolvers and Mauser C/96 pistols.

The Allies were no better off. The standard British army handgun in August 1914 was the six-chambered .455-calibre Webley 'Pistol' Mk IV, which had been adopted in 1899. Though longer barrels are occasionally encountered on officers' guns, the regulation length was 4 inches; the bird's head butt had been inherited from the preceding Mark III, but the revolver was otherwise a standard break-open pattern with an efficient auto-extracting system. Complaints were received from the trenches that the Webley was difficult to grasp with muddied hands. In May 1915, therefore, the Mark VI appeared, with a 6-inch barrel and a new angular grip with a pronounced hump behind the hammer. The lengthened barrel is believed to have been intended to increase the sight radius and hence improve the accuracy of shooting – particularly among subalterns fresh from the playing fields of England.

The Webley was the best combat revolver issued during World War I; it was strong, incorporated a latch preventing the hammer reaching the chambered round unless the breech was properly shut, and had particularly rapid extraction/ejection. The ease with which the Webley could be replenished occupied the thoughts of many inventors, the one tangible result being the introduction of the forerunner of today's speedloaders – Prideaux's Instantaneous Revolver Magazine – in 1915. The Webley was also the only World War I revolver to be fitted with a bayonet, patented by Lieutenant Arthur Pritchard in 1915 and made by W.W. Greener from the blades of old French Gras sword bayonets.

After protracted development, the Webley 'Pistol, Self Loading,

.455 Mark I' (or 'Mark I N') had been adopted by the Royal Navy in 1913. Its action was locked by a barrel lug engaging a corresponding recess in the slide-top. When the gun fired, recoil forced diagonal ribs on the side of the barrel block downwards in grooves cut in the frame side, disengaging the locking lug and allowing the slide to reciprocate. Two locating holes in the magazine back uniquely allowed the entire magazine to be held in reserve while the action was operated as a single loader.

Though Whiting's locking system proved to be sturdy and efficient when clean, it was easily jammed by mud. As the gun was also quite heavy – 2½ pounds unladen – and the grip was much too square to the bore to promote effectual snap-shooting, the Webley autoloader was soon relegated to subsidiary duties. A modification of the original Navy Mark I with a drum-pattern back sight, an auxiliary hammer lock and a shoulder stock was authorized for the Royal Flying Corps in 1915 ('Mark I No.2'), but was soon retired when aircraft machine-guns became commonplace.

The output of Webley Mark VI revolvers was prodigious, the initial government contract asking for 2,500 guns per week for the duration of the war. But even this was insufficient, and the War Office, in desperation, acquired as many .455-chambered Colt and Smith & Wesson revolvers as possible, together with some .455 Colt Government Model semi-automatic pistols. Large numbers of .455 Smith & Wesson-type top-break revolvers – 'Pistol, Old Pattern

The 7.65mm Mo.15/19 pistol helped establish Beretta as an important handgun producer.

with 5-inch Barrel, No.2 Mark I' – were ordered from Garate, Anitua y Cia and Trocaola, Aranzabal y Cia of Eibar, Spain, on 8 November 1915. The Garate y Anitua revolver has 'GAC' monograms on the side of the frame beneath the hammer and on the bakelite grips, the grips are squared off above the protruding bird's head pommel, and the back of the trigger guard tends to be squared; the Trocaola y Aranzabal guns, conversely, have 'TAC' monograms on the frame, their chequered bird's head grips extend to the base of the butt and the trigger-guard backs are almost always rounded. Both patterns were declared obsolete in 1921, the survivors being scrapped or sold at auction.

The problems the British faced were as nothing compared with the experience of the French army. In August 1914, the service handgun was the idiosyncratic 8mm Mle 92, 'Modèle d'Ordonnance' or 'Lebel' revolver (see Chapter 5), which, together with the earlier 11mm Mle 1873, answered immediate needs. Once large-scale mobilisation began in earnest, panic succeeded the realisation that repelling the German armies would not be child's play. Casting around in desperation, the French authorities turned to Spain. The British had already contracted with the best Spanish revolver makers; and, in any case, production of these .455 guns could not have satisfied the French. What was wanted was quantity: quality came a remote second.

The French placed contracts for 8mm-calibre solid-frame swing-out cylinder Smith & Wesson copies; for 7.65mm 'Star' pistols, with highly distinctive open-top slides, from Echeverria y Cia of Eibar; and for 10,000 'Ruby' brand semi-automatic pistols monthly from Gabilondo y Urresti of Guernica. The quantity was soon tripled but, as Gabilondo could not make these nine-shot adaptations of the Mle.1903 FN-Browning in such vast numbers, legions of subcontractors were recruited. Eventually, sixteen companies participated – all supposedly working under Gabilondo y Urresti's control, but in reality doing much as they pleased. However, huge numbers of the guns reached the French and Spanish armies and, after the end of World War I, the newly-formed armies of Yugoslavia and Finland inherited many of the survivors. The 7.65mm Ruby pistols made by the best of the sub-contractors worked adequately, but the worst of them were truly terrible.

In 1914, the Russian army had been content with the obr.1895g revolver ('Nagant Gas-seal'). This had been supplemented prior to 1910 by small numbers of 1903-model FN-Brownings and even a few New Model Parabellums, though the pistols appear to have been reserved for officers, police and internal security units. Many Mauser C/96 pistols had also been acquired by the Tsarist officers. Apart from accelerating production of obr.1895g revolvers in the Tula factory, and rehabilitating surviving Smith & Wesson-type guns (made by Smith & Wesson, Loewe and Tula), the Russians did very little: small numbers of .45 Colt semi-automatics were acquired in 1915-16, along with some Ruby blowbacks diverted from France, but there is no evidence of mass purchasing. The Russian soldiery simply went without handguns.

The Italians had adopted the Mo.910 or 'Glisenti' pistol shortly before the war began, and had been steadily supplementing the existing Mo.1889 ('Bodeo') revolvers. Issue appears to have been to officers and NCOs, leaving the revolvers to the rank and file. Made by Società Siderugica Glisenti and Metallurgica Bresciana gia Temprini (which also made the 'Brixia' derivative for commercial sale), the Mo.910 had a dangerous superficial affinity with the Parabellum. However, its reciprocating bolt was locked by a comparatively weak strut and, as the frame was particularly weak on one side of the magazine well, the 9mm Mo.910 cartridge was appreciably weaker than the 9mm Parabellum. Unfortunately, the two cartridges were dimensionally identical: the German cartridge could easily be fired in the Glisenti, soon straining it irreparably.

The Italians soon discovered that supplies of Glisenti pistols and Bodeo revolvers could neither equip the conscript armies nor cope with the tremendous losses. Large numbers of Ruby-type 7.65mm blowbacks were purchased in Spain in 1915-16. However, the Italians appear to have been more discerning than the French and encouraged the indigenous gunmaking industry to provide alternatives. This inspired Beretta, never previously regarded as a mass-producer of handguns, to develop an efficient little 7.65mm blowback pistol as the 'Mo.915' (or 'Mo.15'). Ordered into immediate mass production, this was to provide the basis of Beretta's subsequent dominance of the Italian pistol market.

Among the minor allies, Belgium had had a selection of sturdy solid-frame Nagant revolvers, together with the FN-Browning blowback pistol models of 1900 and 1903. Most of these, however, had been seized by the Germans after the invasion of Belgium in

1914; the remnants of the Belgian army engaged on the Western Front carried British or French handguns.

When the United States of America was finally drawn into World War I in 1917, the Ordnance Department discovered that having sufficient handguns for the regulars of the American Expeditionary Force was not the same thing as being able to equip a rapidly mobilising reserve, or to account for losses during even a month's combat.

The standard handgun was the .45 Colt M1911 semi-automatic pistol, undoubtedly the best of its type to see service prior to 1918 and destined to emerge with its reputation unsullied at the Armistice. In 1917, however, fewer than 75,000 M1911 pistols – made by Colt and Springfield Armory – were on issue or in store, representing a tenth of the requirement. Mindful of the huge demands being made on Colt, which was still only satisfying a quarter of the demand by the summer of 1917, the Secretary of the Army placed extra contracts for 2.55 million M1911 pistols with Remington, Savage and Winchester, plus several companies with no previous gunmaking experience – from National Cash Register Company of Dayton, Ohio, to Lanston Monotype Company of Philadelphia, Pennsylvania. NCR made cash registers and comptometers; Lanston Monotype made type-casting machinery. By the Armistice, only Remington had delivered guns (13,152 of them), though the formerly Ross-owned Dominion Rifle factory in Quebec, renamed the North American Arms Company, may have assembled

George S. Patton's 1916-vintage .45 Colt Peacemaker was engraved by Cuno Helfricht.

The M1917 Smith & Wesson .45 revolver.

about a hundred early in 1919. The total number of Colt-Brownings on hand on 11 November 1918 amounted to 643,755 against a predicted requirement for about 2.8 million by 1 January 1919!

Though the U.S. Navy, worried that the army would take all available M1911 Colt-Brownings, experimented with several pistols, none was purchased in quantity. Perhaps a dozen 1915-patent recoil-operated .45 Grant-Hammonds were tried in 1917, but the elegant Pedersen-designed hesitation blowback .45 Remington was preferred. However, the war ended before the latter could be standardised as an acceptable substitute in 1919.

SP4 Charles Creel shows the modern competition stance for the Colt M1911A1 pistol.

The U.S. Government also contracted with Colt and Smith & Wesson for revolvers chambering the standard rimless .45 pistol cartridge – which dropped straight through Colt chambers and was retained in some Smith & Wessons only by a shallow ring on which the case mouth could seat. Neither extractor system could work with rimless cases until the advent of the 'Half-moon Clip', designed by Joseph Wesson. Two supporting plates in the cylinder, each containing three rounds, allowed the extractor to function in addition to supporting the cartridges. Colt's New Service and S&W's .44 Hand Ejector revolvers were adapted simply by shortening the back of the cylinder to accommodate the width of the clips. 151,700 eminently serviceable Colts and 153,311 Smith & Wessons were officially purchased between 6 April 1917 and the end of 1918, being known collectively as the 'Model of 1917'.

9. New Beginnings

*What experience and history teach is this — that
people . . . have neither learned anything from history, nor
acted on principles deduced from it.*

Georg Hegel, *Philosophy of History*, 1832

World War I re-drew the map of Europe. Kings had fallen, emperors
had fled; the old order had gone beyond recall. Hungary had gained
independence and much of eastern Germany had been lost to
Poland. Estonia, Latvia and Lithuania proclaimed their freedom;
Finland had shaken off Russian domination after a brief Civil War;
Czechoslovakia had emerged in central Europe; and a wholesale
realignment had occurred in the Balkans, after the formation of
Yugoslavia.

The period between the wars was most notable for the
introduction of new automatic pistols such as the FN-Browning GP
Mle 35. However, they also saw the appearance of snubnose
revolvers such as the Colt Detective Special of 1927 – intended
more for concealment than ballistic efficiency – and the Smith &
Wesson .357 Magnum. Developed from a suggestion by Phillip
Sharpe, the first Magnum was completed on 8 April 1935 and
presented to the then-director of the FBI, J. Edgar Hoover.

By the early 1920s, Germany and Austria had been disarmed
under Allied supervision. Countless firearms had been consigned to
the furnaces – more than 4 million pistols in Germany alone – and
the restriction of the embryo Reichsheer to 100,000 men was easily
satisfied by the remainder. This effectively stifled the German
smallarms industry for a decade, and left the armed forces of the
Weimar Republic with the Parabellum. Though Luger's design
remained accurate, and reliable enough when lubricated, its concept
was very obviously nineteenth-century.

The restrictions prevented the introduction of a new German
service pistol until 1940 (see Chapter 10); instead, the first highly
advanced personal defence pistol, the Walther Polizei-Pistole (PP),
appeared on the market in 1930. Its effectual double-action trigger
system permitted firing – assuming the chamber was loaded –
merely by a simple pull through on the trigger. In most other pistols
apart from the Austro-Bohemian 'Little Tom', designed by Alois
Tomiška and patented immediately after World War I, the hammer
had to be cocked manually for the first shot. The Polizei-Pistole was
very well made and also featured a rotary safety catch on the left
side of the slide which could be used to drop the hammer onto the
chamber. The interposition of the catch-body and a locking firing pin

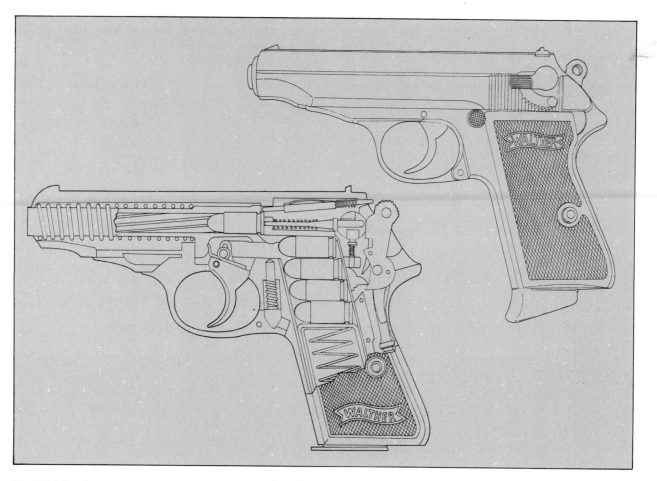

The Walther Polizei-Pistole, patented in 1929, was the first modern double-action blowback.

made this safer than it looked. The PP was adopted as the 'Ehrenwaffe des politischen Leiters' ('honour-weapon of the political leaders') as well as by the police, officers in the armed forces and the paramilitary. It also inspired essentially similar rivals such as the Mauser HSc and the Sauer 38H.

The Austrians retained the excellent Repetierpistole M 12 ('Steyr-Hahn'), spoiled only by the charger-loaded magazine and constructional weakness in the muzzle. That the M 12 chambered a unique cartridge hardly mattered immediately after the Armistice, though most surviving M 12 pistols were converted after the German annexation of Austria (1938) to fire the less powerful 9mm Parabellum cartridge. These have a large 'S' on the left side of the receiver above the grip.

The immediate disbandment of the huge Allied conscript armies left a glut of pistols. Many were scrapped, while others were sold on the commercial market at stupefyingly low prices; consequently, armies of the emerging nations could purchase second-hand guns so cheaply that only the most forward-looking bothered to develop indigenous firearm industries.

The British had been satisfied with the performance of the Webley revolver, but not of the .455 Webley semi-automatic; the Colt M1911 had proved far more effectual in combat. It also became obvious that the .455 cartridge, an awesome manstopper in the hands of an experienced soldier, was ill-suited to conscripts with

A Colt .44 New Service revolver engraved by Rudolf Kornbrath, 1925.

minimal pistol training. Experiments began in the 1920s to devise lightened guns, and the 'Pistol, Revolver, No. 2 Mk 1' ('Enfield') finally appeared in 1932. After spurning the commercially successful .38 Mark IV Webley revolver, the government designers had produced a near-facsimile for British Service! This discreditable episode predictably infuriated Webley & Scott, whose patents had long since expired. During World War II – and another notable shortage of handguns – the Webley .38 Mk IV was, ironically, taken into service alongside the .38/200 'Enfield'.

Experimentation had virtually ground to a halt elsewhere in Europe in the early 1920s. The French were testing several semi-automatic pistols, realizing how singularly ill-prepared they had been when World War I began, but had achieved nothing of consequence. Only in neighbouring Belgium was progress evident. The country's premier smallarms manufacturer, Fabrique Nationale d'Armes de Guerre of Herstal-lèz-Liége, wished to re-establish its once-lucrative pistol exports and soon sold substantial quantities of the new Mle. 10/22 blowbacks to Yugoslavia, The Netherlands and

The Beretta Mo.934 was popular with the Italian troops — and the Fascisti — prior to 1943.

China. Effectual though it was, the Mle. 10/22 did not have the breech-lock necessary to attract major military orders.

The M1911 Colt-Browning pistol had been one of the few completely successful handguns to be issued prior to 1918, and still satisfied the U.S. Army. A few small changes were made in the early 1920s – the hammer spur shape was changed, the mainspring housing was arched and chequered – and the M1911A1 was adopted in September 1926. Immediately after the war, however, John Browning had attempted to improve the Colt and had sought patents on a striker-fired gun with a large-capacity magazine in 1923. Though neither Colt nor the U.S. Army was interested, the Fabrique Nationale management sanctioned a series of prototypes. Unfortunately, on a visit to Herstal in December 1926, before the development programme had been completed, Browning caught a fatal chill. Such was his popularity that virtually every FN employee attended his funeral in Liége.

By the time of Browning's death, several variants of the 1923-patent pistol had been made for trials. An exposed hammer had replaced the original striker mechanism in December 1924, a curious collapsible shoulder stock had been provided, and additional refinements had been made by the time of Browning's demise. Reluctant to abandon such a promising project, FN's design department carried on work under the supervision of Dieudonné Saive. By November 1928, now distinguished by a 13-round staggered-column magazine, the new FN-Browning was all but finished.

At the very moment of triumph came the collapse of Wall Street and the onset of the Depression. It was clearly impossible to spare the capital necessary to invest in mass production, even to re-equip the Belgian army, and the project was deferred until an economic recovery. Finally, in November 1934, the 'Pistolet à Grande

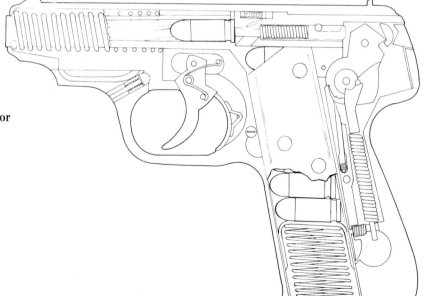

The Sauer M38, an effectual competitor for the Walther Polizei-Pistole.

Puissance, Modèle de 1935' (GP Mle 35) was announced. Adopted immediately by the Belgian army, guns had also been supplied to Estonia and Lithuania prior to 1939. The Chinese army, attempting to expel the Japanese from their territory during the Sino-Japanese War (1937-9), also provided a lucrative market. How the GP Mle 35 eventually equipped Allied and Axis units concurrently is revealed in Chapter 10.

The first emergent nation to produce its own handguns in quantity proved to be Czechoslovakia, whose territory contained the traditional gunmaking centres in Bohemia. After issuing small numbers some uninspiring Praga blowbacks, together with German Ortgies and Dreyse pistols, the Czechs adopted a recoil-operated rotating-barrel design in July 1922. The work of Josef Nickel, once employed by Mauser, the vz.22 soon became the vz.24. The latter remained the standard army handgun until the advent of the curious vz.38 blowback, designed by Frantisek Myška in 1937 and adopted in June 1938. Czech police and internal security services used a simple blowback Nickel-pistol lookalike known as the vz.27.

While the Czechs were perfecting the Nickel pistol, the Japanese, so remote from Europe and the lessons of World War I, prepared a semi-automatic to replace the Meiji 26th Year revolvers and a few remaining Nambu navy pistols. Simplifying the Nambu for mass production resulted in the Taisho 14th Year Type, the first of which were made in Nagoya Army Arsenal in November 1926. The design is usually credited to Nambu alone, but an army commission under his chairmanship was more probably responsible. Nambu resigned his commission in 1924 to form Nambu-jū Seizōshō KK, which then accepted a contract to make 14th Year Types.

Compared with advances being made elsewhere, particularly by Browning, the Japanese pistol has few commendable features. It is, however, better in most respects than the later Type 94 (1934) also generally credited to Nambu, whose company held an exclusive manufacturing contract. The Type 94 sear bar is exposed on the left

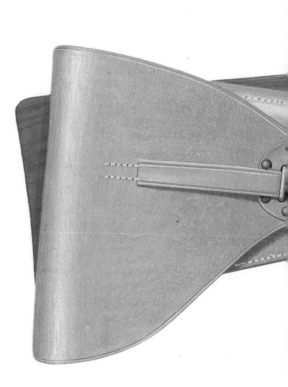

An FN-Browning GP prototype, 1924.

The perfected 9mm FN-Browning GP Mle 35 with its stock and holster.

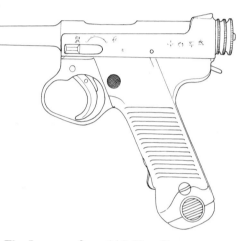

The Japanese 8mm 14th Year Type dated from 1925.

side of the frame, and can be pivoted by a blow – provided the safety catch is off – to fire the gun. The Type 94 had a notoriously weak striker and, like the 14th Year Type, lacked a hold-open; withdrawing the magazine against the pressure of the mainspring can be an acquired skill.

While the Japanese were considering their pistol design, the Bolsheviks were consolidating their hold on post-Revolutionary Russia, after a particularly bloody civil war and embarking on an ambitious programme of economic recovery. Reconstruction of the dilapidated smallarms industry was a priority, as was the development of new designs suited to the crude mass-production at which the Russians excelled. Infantry rifles and light automatic weapons were so important that the first effectual pistol did not appear until 1929 – though Korovin and Prilutskiĭ prototypes had been under test since 1923. The new gun was credited to Fedor Tokarev, who based it on the Government Model Colt-Browning. However, it chambered the 7.63mm Mauser cartridge (which the Russians called '7.62mm'); had its lockwork and hammer assembly carried in a detachable sub-assembly; its magazine feed lips were milled in the frame for maximum efficiency; and it externally resembled the Mle 1903 FN-Browning blowbacks purchased in Tsarist days.

The Pistolet TT ('Tula-Tokarev'), obr. 1930g, was officially adopted in February 1931. Perhaps no more than 1,000 had been made for trials before the design was simplified. True mass-production began in 1934. The Tokarev was never regarded as wholly successful and the obr. 1895g Nagant gas-seal revolver was put back into production while the problems were reviewed. Even as late as 1941, Tokarev pistols and Nagant revolvers were being made in surprisingly similar numbers. The revolver was especially suited to the lowest stratum of illiterate peasant soldiery, and was also used by armoured vehicle crews as the recoiling barrel and slide of the Tokarev were unsuitable for firing-port use. Trials to find a

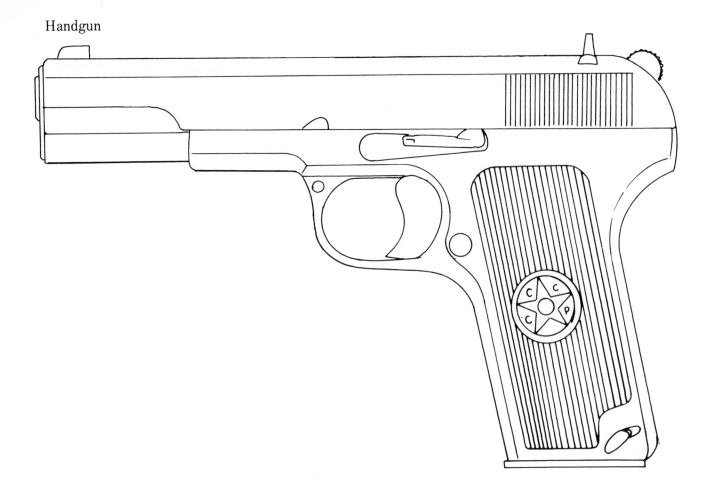

fixed-barrel pistol were still underway when the Germans invaded the Soviet Union in 1941.

Problems with the TT pistol rose more from the inability of Soviet industry to master series production methods rather than any fundamental weakness. Copies made after the end of World War II in Hungary, Yugoslavia and elsewhere have proved that there is nothing inherently wrong with Tokarev's design.

The mid 1930s, once the worst of the Depression had passed, were a particularly interesting period in handgun history: several armies adopted new handguns in 1935 alone. The French had been toying with a series of SE-MAS pistols since 1926, with more enthusiasm than success, until Charles Petter received a patent protecting lockwork 'packaged' on a sub-assembly to facilitate removal. Trials against a SE-MAS blowback and a variant of the GP Mle 35 chambering the odd French 7.65x20mm ('7.65mm Longue') cartridge showed the efficacy of the Petter-Browning, which was standardized as the 'Pistolet Automatique Modèle 1935A'. Production commenced in the Cholet, Alsace, factory of Société Alsacienne de Constructions Mechaniques (SACM) in 1938. Progress was painfully slow, and only 2,700 of the initial order for 10,500 guns had been delivered when the Wehrmacht overran the factory on 23 June 1940.

The French saw the Mle 35A as an expedient, pending development of a simpler version. Dating from 1938, the 'Pistolet

The 7.62mm Tokarev, adopted in 1931, was a minor variant of the Colt-Browning with packaged lockwork and feed lips milled in the frame.

The Polish Radom VIS wz.35, another efficient Browning clone, proved a great favourite with the Wehrmacht.

Modèle 1935S' was just entering production in the Saint-Etienne factory when the Germans invaded France. Only 1,440 Mle 35S pistols had been made. To satisfy post-war French embroilment in Indochina, however, the Mle 35S and Mle 35SM1 were made after *c.*1948 by the government factories in Châtellerault and Tulle, SACM and the privately-owned SAGEM.

The Poles began by issuing ex-Russian Nagant revolvers, and had even bought the old gas-seal revolver production line from Belgium in 1929 after a government decision to purchase rights to the Czech vz.24 pistol had been challenged by Piotr Wilniewczyc, an employee of the National Armaments Factory (PWU). Enlisting the director of the Warsaw machine-gun factory, Jan Skrzypinski, Wilniewczyc quickly perfected a recoil-operated gun in which the barrel lugs were dropped by a cam-way on the frame. Wilniewczyc always acknowledged his debt to Browning, and had probably seen either the 1923 patent or one of the later prototypes made by Fabrique Nationale.

The first Wilniewczyc-Skrzypinski prototype was completed in February 1931, a patent being granted almost exactly a year later. The Polish government (which had been making Nagant revolvers in the interim) then negotiated a licence and adopted the pistol as the 'VIS wz.35', overruling the inventors' request for 'W&S' in favour of 'vis' – the Latin noun for 'force'. The sturdy and effectual wz.35 was the first service pistol to embody a hammer-dropping system controlled by an auxiliary lever on the slide-side.

Finland's L-35 had been designed by Aimo Lahti, the first prototype dating from 1929. Unlike the Browning-principle Petter and wz.35, the Lahti was an eccentric amalgam of the Parabellum (then the standard Finnish service pistol), the Bergmann-Bayard and the Mauser C/96. It bears an external resemblance to the m/23 Parabellum, but lacks the toggle; instead, a rising block in the housing at the rear of the slide secures the bolt when the action is shut. Lahti also included a pivoting accelerator to give an additional thrust to the bolt during the opening stroke.

Interesting design and a reputation for excellent reliability in sub-zero temperatures have gained the Lahti more than its fair share of attention. But it was frighteningly expensive to make and was more a source of national pride than a viable economic project. Though it is popularly assumed that *all* Finns carried L-35 pistols in the Winter War against Russia in 1939-40, the first five guns were delivered in March 1938 and only a little under 500 had been forthcoming by the end of January 1940.

Among the uncommitted and the perennially neutral, Sweden retained the Pistol M/07, a Husqvarna-made FN-Browning Mle 1903 blowback; the Danes had the Pistol m-10/21, a Bergmann Bayard made by Haerens Tøjhus; and the Norwegians, perhaps the best equipped, had the licensed m/1914 Colt-Browning made by the Kongsberg arms manufactory. In the Iberian Peninsula, Portugal retained a collection of Savage and Parabellum pistols while Spain,

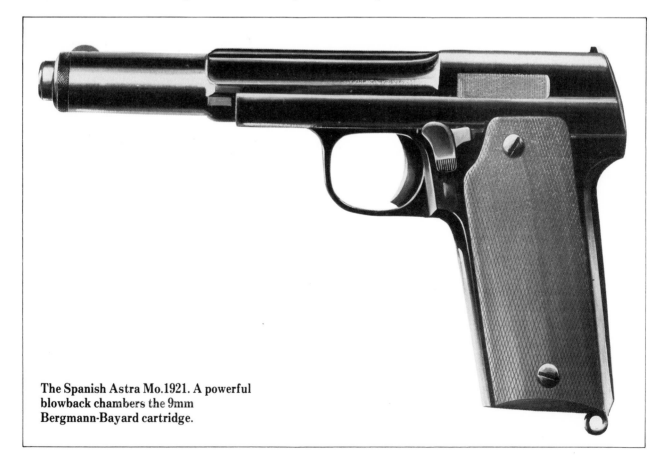

The Spanish Astra Mo.1921. A powerful blowback chambers the 9mm Bergmann-Bayard cartridge.

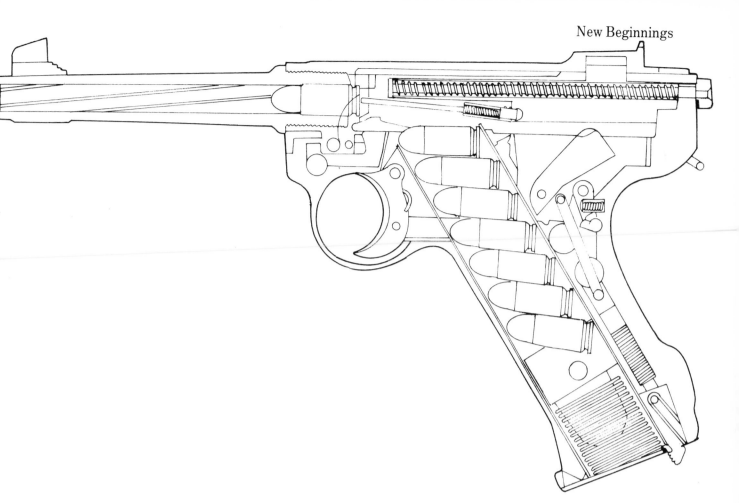

An unusual recoil-operated action characterizes the 9mm Finnish Lahti, adopted in 1935.

having replaced the Bergmann-Mars and Bergmann-Bayard with the indigenous Campo-Giro pistols of 1913 and 1916, had progressed to the Pistola automatica Mo.1921 (marketed commercially as the Astra 400). The most interesting feature of the blowback Mo.1921, apart from its oddly tubular receiver, was that it chambered the powerful 9mm Largo cartridge. This developed greater power than the 9mm Parabellum for which, elsewhere throughout Europe, a locked breech had been considered essential.

The Basque region of northern Spain was the centre of a thriving gunmaking industry, centred on the town of Eibar. Here, at least sixty gunmakers plied their trade until a government decree promulgated at the end of the Spanish Civil War forcibly closed all except Echeverria y Cia, Unceta y Cia and Gabilondo y Cia. Thereafter, even Spain's premier pistol makers operated under rigid government scrutiny.

Prior to 1939, the Spaniards had made a selection of Mauser C/96 lookalikes (Astras, Azuls, Royals), their internal differences belied by their external affinity, together with the blowback Astras and a collection of Colt-Browning copies made under the Star and Llama brands. There were also legions of cheap blowbacks with names such as Destroyer, Martian or Terrible – which described most of them accurately – and revolver designs pirated from Smith & Wesson. Few of these had much military significance, though the fully-automatic pistols sounded impressive enough to catch the eye of the Nicaraguan army and sundry Far Eastern warlords.

10. Return to War

Wars may be fought with weapons, but they are won by men. It is the spirit of the men who follow and of the man who leads that gains the victory.

George S. Patton, *Cavalry Journal*, 1933

The conflict that had scarred the late 1930s in Spain and China, and the territorial ambitions of Hitlerian Germany, plunged Europe into war more frightening in its totality than ever the earlier 'War to End Wars' had been. By 1940, the map of Europe had been forcibly re-drawn once again. The annexation of Austria in 1938 had been followed by the German invasion of Czechoslovakia and Poland. Belgium and The Netherlands had been overrun; France clutched at independence only through the acquiescence of Vichy. An alliance existed between Germany and Italy; the Russo-German non-aggression pact had been signed. Only Britain stood to thwart German ambition. How the British stood firm, bolstered by American aid, and how the German invasion of Russia was checked and ultimately hurled back is now history; by May 1945, war in Europe was over, and the campaigns against Japan would shortly be curtailed by the first atomic bombs.

Compared with atomic bombs, thousand-bomber raids and events as momentous as D-Day, the story of the handgun in World War II has no real significance. But that is not to say that nothing of interest happened.

The immediate problems were not unlike those that had faced the armies during the earlier war; indeed, it is no exaggeration to note

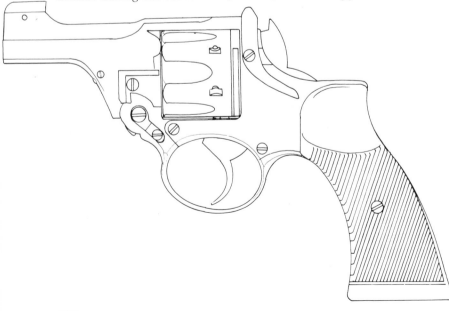

The British .38-calibre No.2 'Enfield' revolver was a minor variant of the Webley.

Adopted in 1940, the 9mm-calibre Walther P.38 only succeeded in replacing the Pistole 08 ('Luger') after the war.

that lessons had gone unheeded. Most efforts, therefore, were initially aimed at increasing production of existing designs.

The British service revolvers were the Enfields, No.2 Marks 1 and 1*. Production exclusively by the Royal Small Arms Factory at Enfield soon proved insufficient and subcontractors were recruited, the most important being Albion Motors Ltd. of Scotstoun, Glasgow, where 24,000 guns were made in 1941-43; and the Singer Sewing Machine Company in Clydesbank, which made components marked SM or SSM. A wartime expedient known as the No.2 Mk 1** was adopted to facilitate production. In addition, the British acquired substantial numbers of .38 Webley Mark 4 revolvers – which were virtually identical with the Enfields – plus Inglis-made GP Mle 35 pistols for commandos and paratroops. Smith & Wesson also supplied large numbers of the .38/200 derivatives of the standard .38 Hand Ejector revolver with wartime-quality finish.

The story of the .38/200 is extraordinary; Smith & Wesson had accepted an order for 9mm Light Rifles from the British Purchasing Commission in the dark days of 1940, but had been unable to make the Light Rifle work satisfactorily. Only a few hundred had been made before the project was abandoned and the British, understandably, requested that the advance monies be returned. As this would have bankrupted Smith & Wesson, company president Carl Hellstrom offered revolvers to the value of the outstanding advance. Production began immediately.

The importance of the handgun in British service was steadily eroded during the war by the Sten Gun, and supplies of Enfields, Webleys, Inglis-Brownings and Smith & Wessons proved sufficient to satisfy most of the needs in all but the darkest months of 1940, when the Local Defence Volunteers (later the Home Guard) sported anything serviceable.

The Germans, embroiled on so many fronts, required millions of guns to equip not only the Wehrmacht but also the paramilitary, police and occupation forces. When war commenced, the official German service pistol was still the venerable P.08 (Parabellum). However, experiments with a recoil-operated double action Walther

Heeres-Pistole culminated in the introduction of the P.38 in April 1940. Despite being made by Walther, Mauser and Spreewerke, plus several subcontractors, the P.38 merely supplemented the Parabellum in German service.

Production of more than 2.5 million P.08 and P.38 during the Third Reich failed to satisfy the demands, and the Germans impressed not only the advanced double-action personal defence pistols for which they were fast becoming famous – Walther PP/PPK series, Mauser HSc, Sauer M38 – but also guns seized in Belgium, The Netherlands, Poland, Czechoslovakia, France and Norway. In addition, production continued in as many facilities as possible and guns were bought in Hungary and ostensibly neutral (but actually pro-Axis) Spain. Guns such as the Walther PP were particularly prized as officers' weapons, but were also extensively carried by aircrew owing to their small size.

Many differing pistols will be found with Waffenamt marks. Issued under their fremdgeräte numbers, which referred to a list compiled by German Intelligence services prior to the war. The most prized were the Pistole 35(p) and the Pistole 640(b) – the wz.35 'Radom' and the Fabrique Nationale-made GP Mle 35. These powerful 9mm Browning-system guns were issued to combat troops wherever possible, though many Radoms went to the Kriegsmarine. The 7.65mm Pistole 626(b) and 37(u) – the FN-Browning Mle.10/22 and Hungarian 37.M blowbacks – generally went to the Luftwaffe. Between January 1939 and February 1945, more than 3.73 million pistols were acquired.

A law under which all civilian pistols had to be surrendered for possible military use had been passed in Germany in 1938. These guns were then inspected by the Waffenamt inspectors and, in many cases, reissued; consequently, German ordnance marks may be found on improbable semi-automatics such as the Belgian Armand Gavage.

Operation 'Barbarossa', the German invasion of Russia, so damaged the Soviet smallarms industry that production virtually halted while the factories were entrained and re-erected eastward. The principal Soviet handguns remained the Tokarev pistol and the Nagant gas-seal revolver, as experiments to find replacements for the former were still incomplete. The several hundred thousand Russian pistols made in 1941-5, plus surviving 6.35mm Tula-Korovin blowbacks serving officers, police and party officials, appear to have satisfied the demands made on them. However, as the war dragged on, these handguns were subordinated to the submachine-gun.

Elsewhere in Europe, the Italians continued to use the Mo.934 Beretta blowback – together with many earlier serviceable Beretta or Glisenti pistols and Bodeo revolvers. The comparatively limited sphere of operations and the early departure of Italy from the war, however, minimized supply problems. Portugal and Spain remained neutral, being equipped largely with Parabellum (9mm Mo. 909 and Mo.943) and Astra (Mo.1921) pistols respectively, though the Portuguese Guardia Nacional Republicana had the 7.65 mm Mo.935 Parabellum and the Spanish Guardia Civil used the Mo. 1922

The GP35 copy made by Inglis of Toronto was popular with British commandos and airborne forces.

Pistols were generally reduced to minor roles in World War II. The commander of this German machine-gun crew wears a P.08 holster alongside his bayonet.

Browning-type Star. Sweden retained the Pistol M/07, a Husqvarna-made FN-Browning blowback, though trials undertaken in 1937-9 had led to the adoption of the Walther Heeres-Pistole as the M/39. When the war began, and no more Walthers would be forthcoming from Germany, the Swedes fell back on their third choice – the Finnish Lahti – as the German invasion of Belgium had removed the second choice, the FN GP Mle 35. Adopting the Lahti was a popular move, as many pro-Finnish Swedes had disapproved of their government's strict neutrality during the Winter War. Unfortunately, the Husqvarna-made Lahti was never as successful as the Finnish L-35.

The enforced removal of Fabrique Nationale from the export markets prevented GP Mle 35 pistols reaching the Chinese army after 1940. However, several members of the FN design staff escaped to Britain with a set of blueprints and a few pistol samples. The technicians finally settled in Canada, where the government had contracted with the John Inglis Company of Toronto to make GP pistols alongside Bren Guns; Inglis subsequently made about 151,800 'Pistols, Browning, FN' No.1 and No.2 for the Chinese, Canadian and British armies. Owing to the large magazine capacity, the Inglis-Browning was very popular with Anglo-Canadian commandos and airborne troops. Ironically, after the invasion of Normandy in 1944, many FN-made guns were retrieved from the German forces by invaders carrying the Inglis-made equivalent – perhaps the only instance of an automatic pistol, made by two different companies, being issued by opposing sides simultaneously.

The U.S. Army was still satisfied with the M1911A1 Colt-Browning when the Japanese bombed Pearl Harbor in December

Corporals Jaggie, Riesenberg and Blake
demonstrate firing the three principal
service weapons from the hip. Blake, on
the right, has an M1911A1.

1941. As soon as mobilisation commenced, the authorities encountered the age-old problem: too few guns for too many reservists. The new .30 M1 Carbine was to arm many former pistoleers, but it was soon obvious that production of the M1911A1 would need to be quadrupled owing to delays with the Carbine. Colt had already been requested to make guns as fast as possible, supplementary orders for 50,000 dating back prior to Pearl Harbor. The Ordnance Department had also approached the Singer Manufacturing Company in Elizabethport, New Jersey, where a duplicate production line had been installed under Colt's supervision in 1940. Rather oddly, Singer made only 500 pilot guns before work ceased. In 1942, three new contractors were recruited: Union Switch & Signal Company of Swissvale, Pennsylvania; Ithaca Gun Company of Ithaca, New York; and Remington Rand, Inc., of New York. By the end of the war, Colt and Ithaca had each made about 400,000, with a further 50,000 from Union Switch & Signal. But Remington-Rand managed no less than 900,000, for a grand total of about 1.8 million. Virtually all wartime M1911A1 pistols featured plastic grips and matt phosphated finish, rather than the pre-war wood and polished blue.

Few developments were made in U.S. handguns during the war as supplies of M1911A1 pistols, M1 Carbines and non-military pistols and revolvers proved adequate. However, the Guide Lamp Division of General Motors made large numbers of a single-shot manually operated 'throwaway' pistol, designed by the OSS as the '.45 Flare Projector' but popularly known as the Liberator. A million of these guns, each packed with 10 .45 ACP cartridges and a sheet of very graphic instructions, were made in three months. They were to be air-dropped to European partisans. The Liberator was to be supplemented by the improved 'Deer Gun', but the war finished before anything other than prototypes had been made. A pressed and stamped derivation of the M1911A1 was Guide Lamp's contribution to the simplified construction principles embodied in the German Volkspistolen described below.

The Japanese produced the pre-war 14th Year Type and Type 94 pistols throughout the war, few changes being made other than to

The cheap single-shot Liberator was destined for European Resistance personnel.

simplify production. 14th Year Types made after about 1939 will be encountered with a large trigger guard, said to have been added to permit a gloved finger on the trigger. These guns are usually known in the West as the 'Kiska' model after the Aleutian island on which the first examples were captured, though the change was due to combat experience in Manchuria. By 1945, Japanese industry had been so dislocated by American bombing that the quality of the pistols had become truly awful. Fearful of the impending U.S. Army invasion, the Japanese had also produced substantial numbers of one-shot hinawa-jū (or 'fire-rope guns') with bamboo or crude iron tube barrels bound with cord for additional strength; mercifully for the firers, these pale imitations of a four-hundred year tradition were never needed. Quite apart from the undesirability of facing U.S. troops carrying Garands or M1 Carbines with matchlocks, the hinawa-jū held more danger to the firer than the intended target.

Though the German arms industry never plumbed the depths of its Japanese equivalent, the development of an assortment of Volkspistolen in 1944-45 also smacked of desperation. Unlike the Japanese matchlocks, the German emergency pistols were nonetheless interesting design concepts. Walther made a pressed-steel high power prototype with a rotating barrel lock, probably in early 1944 and then graduated to an all-metal PP derivative; Mauser made a selection of guns, some blowback and others incorporating delay; and Gustloff-Werke of Suhl also contributed a delayed blowback pattern. The best of these designs was to be made by the hundred thousand for last-ditch facing the inevitable Russian invasion, but the war ended before a suitable gun could be found.

Apart from the standard guns, and the one-shot specials, silenced pistols were made for the Office of Strategic Services, the Special Operations Executive and other agencies to whom stealth was second nature. High-Standard HD-U.S.A. .22 rimfire training pistols were modified to accept silencers for the O.S.S., and the S.O.E. designers in Welwyn, Hertfordshire, developed the 'Welrod' silenced pistol – or Hand Firing Device Mk 1 – in 1943. These influenced post-war Chinese 'assassination' designs appreciably.

11. Modern Times

It's the world's newest, most advanced single action/double action fighting handgun . . . You can dunk it, soak it, wash it, dry it and it will come out shooting. The ultimate combat pistol. Simply The Best.

Sales claims for the abortive Mamba pistol, *c.*1980

Very little handgun experimentation was undertaken during World War II, and, in many armies, the submachine-gun had greatly reduced the status of the pistol. Apart from the Volkspistolen, the simplified construction of which the Allies examined with interest, only Switzerland had achieved much.

The standard Swiss service handgun in 1940 had been the Ordonnanzpistole 06/29 W + F, one of the last Parabellums to be adopted. In the late 1930s, however, Schweizerische Industrie-Gesellschaft (SIG) of Neuhausen had purchased a licence for the French Petter pistol, and the SIG SP 44/8 and 44/16 – the latter with a 16-round magazine – successfully outperformed the government's Pistole 43 W + F Browning and Pistole 47 W + F in protracted trials. The perfected SIG SP 47/8 was adopted as the Ordonnanzpistole 49 in 1949. Offering the excellent quality befitting its origins, the SIG-Petter was a standard tipping-barrel Browning with its slide carried on external frame rails to provide an unusually lengthy bearing surface. Excellent accuracy and reliability were among its assets.

The SP 47/8 was subsequently adopted by Denmark and the West German border guards, but was too expensive to attract large-volume sales. Simplification of the basic design in the 1970s has now provided a series of guns made by SIG and marketed in collusion with J.P. Sauer of Eckenförde, West Germany. The SIG-Sauer P220, P225 and P226 have proved durable and efficient; sales to the German state police have been very good, and the P226 came a close second to the Beretta 92F in the U.S. pistol trials. The SIG-Sauer pistols feature a variant Browning-type tipping barrel lock in which the locking shoulder on the barrel simply rises into an enlarged ejection port in the slide.

With the forcible removal of German guns from the commercial market after 1945 – perhaps preventing the Walther P.38 being a global success – the FN-Browning GP Mle 35 cornered much of the market; before production ceased in 1987, it had been sold to more than 60 countries. Surprisingly few changes have been made in the basic gun, the introduction of a 'Mark 2' being largely cosmetic. The

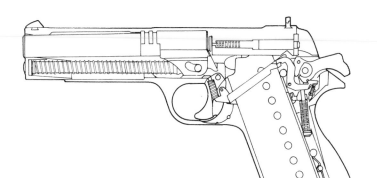

The expensive SIG SP-210 is regarded as one of the best-made and most efficient of all semi-automatic pistols.

basic fixed-sight model was latterly known as the Vigilant; the Captain had a tangent-leaf back sight and a shoulder-stock cut in the butt; the Sport featured modified sights and chequered walnut grips; and engraved guns featured Renaissance and Louis XVI-style decoration.

The incorporation of so much of Eastern Europe in the Soviet bloc ended firearms development in Poland, though the Czechs retained more independence. Though the Soviet bloc initially equipped with variations of the Tokarev obr. 1930g pistol, made in several of the Russian satellites, the Czech army accepted the vz.52 after experimenting with its ČZ 491 and ČZ 513 prototypes in 1950-52. The ČZ design was an adaptation of the roller-locked action of the German MG. 42 machine-gun. Unlike the later Heckler & Koch P9, which is a delayed blowback, the vz.52 breech is rigidly locked at the moment of firing.

Shortly after the vz.52 had entered service, the Russians produced the 9mm Pistolet Makarova (PM), a small double-action blowback freely adapted from the German Walther PP, and the comparatively unsuccessful Avtomaticheskaia Pistolet Stechkina (APS), a large blowback capable of selective fire. Apparently issued to internal security units rather than the army, the 20-shot Stechkin is rather too light to control when firing at 750 rounds per minute,

Above: The 9mm Russian Stechkin could fire fully automatically, but was not especially successful.

Above: The SIG P225 is one of the latest derivatives of the SP-210 series.

even with its wood-body holster-stock. Both Russian guns fire a special 9x18mm cartridge whose dimensions are such that they will also chamber 9mm Short and 9mm Police cartridges – though Western 9mm Auto/9mm Police examples will *not* chamber the Russian round.

Though interesting, fully-automatic pistols still prove a dead-end in handgun development, and interest has switched to burst-firers such as the Heckler & Koch VP70 and the Beretta 951R and 93 series.

The Italians, having pulled out midway through the war and deposed Mussolini, were more favoured by the Allies than Germany. Consequently, little objection was raised when Beretta

Right: The Beretta 92-F (9mm Pistol M9) was adopted by the U.S. Army in 1985.

wished to resume handgun production. Realising that the pre-war Mo.34 blowback would not attract military orders, the company, by adapting the operating system of the Walther P.38, produced an elegant recoil-operated pistol known as the Mo.951 or 'Brigadier'. Problems with the original alloy frame delayed mass production of this gun, but it subsequently proved most successful. After being adopted officially in Italy and Egypt, a programme of continuous development led to the Mo. 951R, which was capable of firing bursts of three shots, and then to the current '92' (semi-automatic) and '93' (selective-fire) series. The U.S. Army adopted the Beretta 92F as the '9mm Pistol M9' in 1985, replacing the legendary .45 M1911A1, and the 92F has now overcome its rivals to win the French army trials of 1986-7. As Fabrique Nationale has a substantial stake in Beretta, it is interesting to speculate that the Beretta will be the 'GP' of the late twentieth century now that the latter has been discontinued.

The Beretta is unremarkable mechanically, which seems typical of all globally successful pistols. It relies on a propped-up block

Right: **The Soviet PSM pistol, intended purely for personal defence, chambers an unusual 6.45mm-calibre cartridge.**

below the breech to lock the action, recoil moving the barrel/slide group back far enough to cam the locking block downwards off its plateau. This releases the slide which, when the barrel halts against the frame, reciprocates alone to cock the hammer and strip a fresh round into the breech on the return stroke. Though the early Beretta 951 was generally considered weaker than the P.38, the problem has been solved, otherwise the endurance trials would have proved their undoing.

Walther was prevented from making the P.38 until 1957, by which time the export markets were satisfied by the FN-Browning

MODELE 250
CAL.9mm

Above: **The 9mm French MAC 1950 pistol was based on pre-war Petters.**

GP and, to a lesser degree, the Beretta Mo.951; initial sales of the P.38 were confined to the Bundeswehr. The modern gun differs little from its wartime predecessor, excepting in the design of the safety catch and firing pin, and has proved as successful as could be expected in the circumstances. The slides of early guns sometimes fractured where the manufacturer's marks had been rolled-in, and a strengthened (star-marked) pattern appeared in the 1960s. Realising that the P1, as the P.38 had been renamed in 1963, was being overtaken by many more modern designs, Walther produced the shortened P4 before proceeding to the greatly refined P5. The P5 – which has a full-length slide though otherwise internally pure Walther – performed well enough in the German pistol trials of 1973-5 to be adopted by the police forces of Baden-Württemberg and Rheinland-Palatinate, and has subsequently been purchased by the Royal Netherlands Police.

The German police trials failed to separate the P5, P6 and P7 – the Walther, SIG-Sauer and Heckler & Koch – and purchasing decisions were left to the individual states. As the P5 proved least popular, Walther abandoned the 1935-vintage locking system in favour of the P88. In this, an adaptation of the classic Walther double-action trigger mechanism has been amalgamated with a Browning-type tipping barrel. The P88 apparently performed very well in the recent French trials, losing to the Beretta partly because it had no record of mass production and partly because Beretta offered an excellent after-sale package. But the progress of the new Walther may be worth watching.

The rise of Heckler & Koch of Oberndorf, Württemberg, has been one of the most notable features of the post-war West German arms industry. H&K began by making the roller-locked G3 rifle, developed in Spain from wartime Mauser designs, but then adapted the basic principle to an autoloading pistol known as the P9. Credited to Herbert Meidel, the P9 and P9S feature an interesting roller-delayed blowback action and polygonal rifling. Like many German pistols, however, they remained very complicated; typically, H&K then sought something different. The result was the P7, a gas-delayed blowback with a unique squeeze-cocking grip. Other projects have included the short-lived VP70 and VP70Z, large 18-shot blowbacks incorporating three-shot burst firing capabilities. The burst-firing selector was incorporated in the synthetic shoulder stock to prevent the detached pistol being used in any way but conventionally.

The crippling restrictions placed on handguns in Britain have prevented much innovation; even the Webley revolvers disappeared from the market in the late 1960s. In the U.S.A., however, work has continued unabated. Though the M1911A1 has finally been superseded by the Beretta 92F (as the Pistol M9), there are many who regard the .45 ACP as a better combat round than the 9mm Parabellum and Colt will undoubtedly continue its wide range of Browning-type guns: Government Model, Combat Commander, Lightweight Commander, Officer's ACP, 380 Government Model, Mustang 380, Gold Cup National Match, and now the new .45 ACP Combat Elite and 10mm-calibre Delta Elite. A sizable industry in the U.S.A. is still based on the M1911A1; some companies simply customize old guns, but others are actually making new ones. Typical of these are Arminex, Randall Firearms and MS Safari Arms.

During the late 1960s, Colt engineer Robert Roy developed an improved double-action 'Model 1971' variant of the basic M1911A1. Patented in August 1972, the project lay dormant until U.S.A.F. interest revived in 1977. Unfortunately, the performance of the SSP ('Stainless Steel Pistol') was poorer than rivals such as the SIG-Sauer and Beretta, and the gun was abandoned. Licensed to ODI in the early 1980s, the SSP is now being marketed as the .45 Auto Viking Combat.

Smith & Wesson, better known for its revolvers, demonstrated the first prototype Browning-type P.38 inspired double-action pistol in October 1948; however, interest was minimal, and though the U.S. Army requested a few single-action guns, production did not begin until December 1954. Not until the end of the decade did S&W

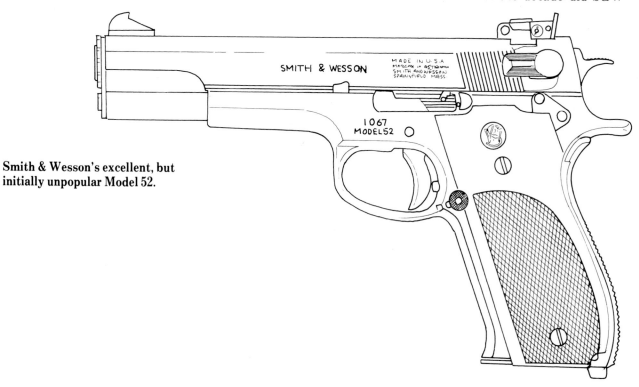

Smith & Wesson's excellent, but initially unpopular Model 52.

149

The pick of today's pistols include the Walther P5 (1); the Glock 17 (2); the IMI Desert Eagle (3); the Heckler & Koch P7 (4); the Smith & Wesson M469 (5); and the CZ75 (6).

3

6

manage to sell Model 39 pistols in quantity. The fourteen-shot Model 59, developed in 1964-9, went into production in 1971; the current range includes the M439 (9mm, eight-shot), M459 (9mm, fourteen-shot) and compact M469 Mini-Gun (9mm, twelve-shot). The Models 639, 659 and 669 are stainless-steel versions of the standard guns, and the new M645, a 639 chambering the .45 ACP cartridge, is proving popular with U.S. police forces, owing to its large calibre.

The decision of the U.S. Army to adopt the Beretta was controversial, and Smith & Wesson has been fighting since 1985 to overturn it. The campaign of invective and innuendo has rather obscured the facts, and the true story has yet to emerge. It would be ironic, should the trials recommence, if the new Ruger P-85 proves more acceptable than the Smith & Wesson.

Ruger's is the great success story of the post-1945 U.S. firearms industry, making a series of excellent rifles and handguns ranging from .22 rimfire blowbacks to sturdy revolvers such as the .22 Bearcat (replaced by the New Model Single Six) and the mighty .44 Redhawk. The Security Six has proved popular with police, and the mantle seems destined to fall on the new GP-100. During the late 1970s, the company began work on a Browning-type tipping barrel pistol with a double-action lock.The perfected P-85 appeared in the mid 1980s; shorter and possibly handier than the Beretta, this Ruger may yet prove to be a U.S. service handgun.

The American scene has often featured 'the ultimate pistol', most of which fail after a few years. The awesome .44 Auto-Mag, designed in 1969, was introduced in 1971 and then made by a bewildering variety of manufacturers until disappearing in the mid 1970s; the gas-operated Wildey, designed by W.J. Moore in 1973-5, failed to find market acceptance; and the currently-defunct Bren-Ten, a potentially excellent .40-calibre Browning-type double action pistol

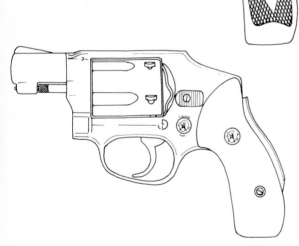

Three Smith & Wesson revolvers: the Models 37 (top), 38 (middle) and 40 (bottom).

credited to Jeff Cooper, failed more through shaky finance and promotion than inherent faults. The demise of the Bren-Ten is by no means uncommon, as effectual funding is vital to compete successfully against Colt, Smith & Wesson and Ruger.

The success of double-action 9mm large-capacity pistols has inspired a number of Spanish designs, the most successful of which appears to be the Astra A-80/A-90 series, though the Star 28 and the American-designed Llama Omni may still hold promise. Among the best of the European designs, however, is the Czech ČZ75 – which has interested the West so greatly that it has been copied in Switzerland, as the ITM AT84, and a modified variant (the Tanfoglio TA-90) has appeared in Italy. Another potentially excellent Italian design is the Bernadelli P-18 Browning-pattern double action pistol.

The interesting Israeli-made IMI Desert Eagle, also apparently originating in the U.S.A., is gas- rather than recoil-operated and represents a departure from the Browning tipping-barrel standard throughout the modern pistol industry. Chambering .357 or .44 Magnum, the Desert Eagle is one of the many impressive designs launched in a blaze of publicity; its long-term success is, however, by no means assured.

Increasing interest in the large-bore military automatic has been accompanied by a revival in the fortunes of the double-action personal defence pistol typified by the Walther PP (which is still in production after more than fifty years). However, though copied by many of the smaller U.S. gunmakers and made under licence by Interarms, the Walther is comparatively expensive, and many

The .38 Colt Detective Special,
originally introduced in 1927 but
extensively revised several times.

purchasers favour appreciably cheaper Spanish Astra or Argentine
Bersa rivals. The most recent '80' series Berettas are particularly
appealing; licensed to Fabrique Nationale as the FN Mle 140 DA,
they may be obtained in a number of differing finishes, chambering
and magazine capacities.

Though the pistol has made considerable inroads in the
commercial market – particularly in Europe – the revolver is still
more popular in the U.S.A., where it has traditionally been the
weapon of the police and has only recently been challenged by Smith
& Wesson's pistols. Consequently, Colt and Smith & Wesson have
both produced excellent guns since World War II. These have
included the S&W Model 29, developed in 1954 for Remington's
impressive .44 Magnum cartridge and introduced in December 1955.
Though developed on the advice of pundits such as the late Elmer
Keith, the .44 Magnum owes most of its current reputation to the
Clint Eastwood film *Dirty Harry*. And while the .357 and .44
Magnum revolvers proved very successful, the 1963-vintage .41
Magnum Model 57 has proved much less popular. The present S&W
production encompasses old faithfuls such as the Model 10 Military
& Police, whose origins date back to 1899, alongside the
Distinguished Combat Magnum series (561, 586, 681 and 686), the
first of which appeared in 1981.

Post-1945 Colts have included the snubnose Aircrewman of 1950,
replaced by the Agent in 1962, together with the Trooper (1954) and
the Python (1855). As a result of public demand, the legendary
Single Action Army or Peacemaker was even put back into

The Ruger .44 Redhawk.

production in 1956. Current products include the legendary Python and its derivative, the Diamondback, together with the Trooper Mk V and Lawman Mk V (1982) and the essentially similar Peacekeeper, which appeared in 1985. These co-exist with the Detective Special and the plain-finish Agent, the latter being introduced in 1964, though the modern guns differ considerably from their similarly-named predecessors. Colt has even offered Italian-made re-creations of its original percussion revolvers.

Rugers such as the Security Six, Single Six, Speed Six and GP-100 have proved very popular for personal defence and police use, while larger revolvers such as the Blackhawk and Redhawk – in .30 M1 Carbine, .357 and .44 Magnum – have proved just as effectual in the field. Ruger should be considered as an equal of Colt and Smith & Wesson. Other U.S. revolvers include the competitively-priced Harrington & Richardson rimfires and the Charter Arms series; while Brazilian Taurus and Argentine Rossi examples, generally based on Smith & Wesson practice, are often comparable with the North American products.

European revolver makers are fewer. Excellent guns are

Dirty Harry's gun: the mighty Smith & Wesson Model 29, .44 Magnum.

A .357 Magnum Colt Python.

This French Manurhin MR-73 is one of the best European revolvers.

produced by Manurhin in France, a wider (but cheaper) Arminius range emanates from Weihrauch in Germany, and Bernadelli still makes S&W-type revolvers in Italy. The most desirable of all are the expensive but beautifully-made West German Korths, recognisable by full-length under-barrel ejector rod shrouds and a cylinder release catch behind the hammer.

The U.S. market has a penchant for strange guns such as the Dardick and the Gyrojet. Patented in the early 1950s, the former fired conventional .38 Special cartridges encased in triangular synthetic carriers. These were indexed in a special 'cylinder' above the box magazine, allowing the promoters to claim the advantages of a magazine pistol with the mechanical simplicity of a revolver. However, the Dardick was too curious to attract success. Marketed

This .22-calibre Hämmerli 232 is typical of modern rapid-fire target pistols.

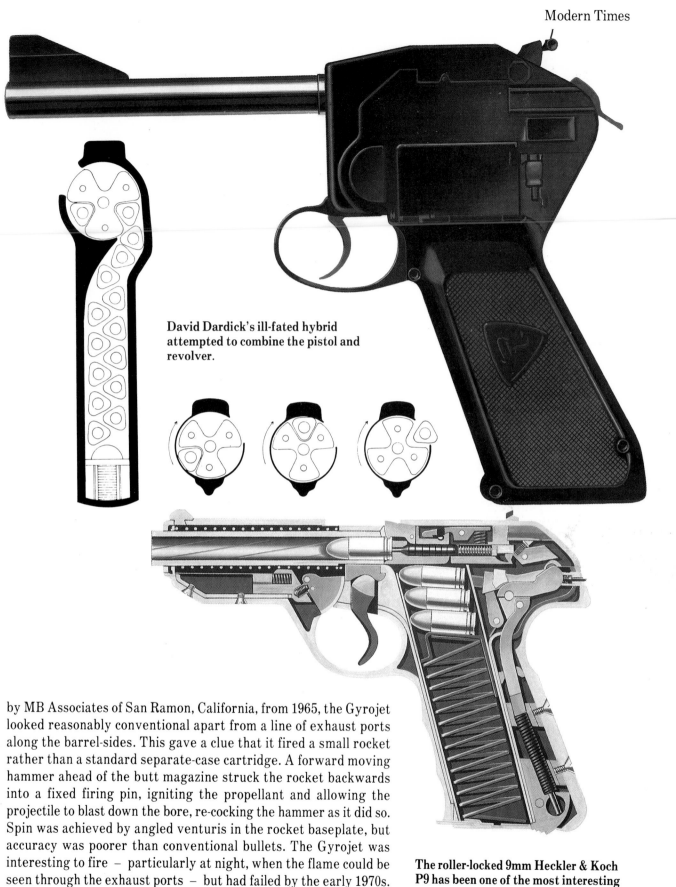

David Dardick's ill-fated hybrid attempted to combine the pistol and revolver.

by MB Associates of San Ramon, California, from 1965, the Gyrojet looked reasonably conventional apart from a line of exhaust ports along the barrel-sides. This gave a clue that it fired a small rocket rather than a standard separate-case cartridge. A forward moving hammer ahead of the butt magazine struck the rocket backwards into a fixed firing pin, igniting the propellant and allowing the projectile to blast down the bore, re-cocking the hammer as it did so. Spin was achieved by angled venturis in the rocket baseplate, but accuracy was poorer than conventional bullets. The Gyrojet was interesting to fire – particularly at night, when the flame could be seen through the exhaust ports – but had failed by the early 1970s. It is unlikely that the principle will be resurrected, current research concentrating more on caseless rounds than miniature rockets.

The roller-locked 9mm Heckler & Koch P9 has been one of the most interesting guns of recent years.

Current oddities include the single-shot Ljutic Space Gun, which competes with more conventional single-shot dropping-block designs offered by Thompson/Center Arms ('Contender'), MCA Group ('Maximum Single Shot') and Rock Pistol Manufacturing Company ('Merrill Sportsman'), plus the well-established bolt-action Remington XP-100. The strangest of all guns, however, are some of the .22 rimfire single-shot Free Pistols which – despite traditions founded in the elegant duelling pistols of the eighteenth century – now feature hand-enveloping grips, spirit levels and bizarre counterweights. ISU rules are periodically revised to eliminate the greatest freaks such as the Soviet MTsZ-1 rapid-fire pistol, which was banned after taking a gold medal at the 1956 Melbourne Olympic Games. Its inverted action had permitted an unusually low barrel axis, currently fashionable but then regarded as an unfair advantage.

The MBA Gyrojet fired tiny rockets, but poor accuracy caused its downfall.

The Mini-Uzi is typical of the many attempts to reduce submachine-guns to handgun proportions.

Index

References to illustrations are
in *italic*.